Shanghai
Financial Services Workforce
Statistics Report 2018

上海金融行业从业人员
统计调查报告2018

上海市金融工作局 著

上海人民出版社

Contents

目　录

Contents

综　述

　　建设上海国际金融中心是一项重大国家战略，其中人才因素至关重要。为全面、准确地了解和掌握本市金融行业从业人员的总体情况和结构分布，为进一步研究制定促进金融机构、金融人才集聚和发展的相关政策提供依据，中共上海市金融工作委员会、上海市金融服务办公室、上海市统计局于 2015 年首次在全市范围内联合开展上海金融人才情况调查，调查对象是在沪注册的金融机构在上海地区从事金融活动的从业人员，并根据调查成果形成了《上海金融人才调查报告 2015》。2018—2020 年是上海"基本建成与我国经济实力以及人民币国际地位相适应的国际金融中心"的决胜阶段，新的战略发展目标对上海金融行业从业人员的总量规模和能力素质提出了新的更高要求。为摸清当前上海金融行业从业人员"家底"，更新相关统计调查数据，为持续推进金融机构、金融人才集聚和发展，建设国际金融人才高地提供政策参考依据，中共上海市金融工作委员会、上海市金融工作局于 2018 年再次联合市统计局在全市范围内开展了金融行业从业人员统计调查工作，并根据最新统计调查成果形成了《上海金融行业从业人员统计调查报告 2018》。

一、调查对象

（一）金融机构

纳入本次统计调查的单位是截至 2017 年 12 月 31 日在上海注册的金融机构，按照行业管理体系分为七大类，即全国性金融市场和基础设施，银行业金融机构，证券业金融机构，保险业金融机构，银行卡清算、支付结算和征信机构，国际金融组织以及地方金融机构。

第一类：全国性金融市场和基础设施

包括上海证券交易所、上海期货交易所、中国金融期货交易所、中国外汇交易中心、上海黄金交易所、上海保险交易所、上海票据交易所、上海清算所、中国信托登记有限公司、中央国债登记结算公司上海总部、中国证券登记结算公司上海分公司、跨境银行间支付清算（上海）公司等。

第二类：银行业金融机构

1. 银行类金融机构：包括政策性银行、国有银行、股份制商业银行、城市商业银行、农村商业银行、村镇银行、外资银行、民营银行、持牌营运中心（资金营运中心、票据营业部、私人银行部、贵金属业务部、人民币交易业务总部、信用卡中心、小企业金融服务中心）、上海总部、金融科技公司（数据中心、软件中心等）；

2. 非银行金融机构：包括信托公司、货币经纪公司、消费金融公司、金融租赁公司、集团财务公司、汽车金融公司、金融资产投资公司等。

第三类：证券业金融机构

1. 证券公司：包括注册在沪的证券公司、异地证券公司在沪分支机构（营业部）、证券投资咨询公司、证券承销保荐子公司 、证券自营、证券类资产管理公司等；

2. 期货公司：包括注册在沪的期货公司、异地期货公司在沪分支机构（营业部）等；

3. 公募基金类企业：包括基金公司（公募）、基金子公司、基金销售机构等；

4.私募基金管理人：包括管理规模在 10 亿元以上的私募股权（含 QFLP）、私募证券、其他（含 QDLP）等。

第四类：保险业金融机构

包括保险集团、人寿保险公司、财产保险公司、再保险公司、养老保险公司、健康保险公司、农业保险公司、上海总部、保险经纪与代理公司、保险公估公司、航运保险营运中心、保险类资产管理公司、自保公司等。

第五类：银行卡清算、支付结算和征信机构

1.银行卡清算机构；

2.第三方支付机构；

3.金融类征信机构。

第六类：国际金融组织

包括金砖国家新开发银行、全球清算对手方协会（CCP12）等。

第七类：地方金融机构

1.小额贷款公司；

2.融资性担保公司；

3.区域性股权市场；

4.典当行；

5.融资租赁公司；

6.商业保理公司；

7.地方资产管理公司。

（二）从业人员

纳入本次统计调查的从业人员是截至 2017 年 12 月 31 日在上述金融机构中从事劳动并直接取得劳动报酬或经营收入的全部人员。包括在岗职工、劳务派遣人员及其他从业人员，不包括：离开本单位仍保留劳动关系，并定期领取生活费的人员；在本单位实习的各类在校学生；本单位的参军人员；本单位因劳务外包而使用的人员。

二、调查方法

本次调查采用了重点调查和抽样调查相结合的方法，其中对从业人员

数在 100 人及以上的金融机构进行重点调查，对从业人员数在 100 人以下的金融机构进行抽样调查。

三、调查内容

本次调查主要包括两部分内容：一是金融机构基本情况，含单位名称、单位所在地地址、单位所在地代码、单位注册地址、登记注册地代码、邮政编码、金融类别等；二是从业人员基本情况，含从业人员年末人数、年龄、文化程度、职称、获得职业水平认证人数、获得职业准入资格人数、从业人员流动情况等。

四、特别说明

根据上海市统计局发布的数据，截至 2017 年末，上海金融行业从业人员总数为 35.54 万人 [①]。本次统计调查及研究分析的对象是金融行业中最具代表性的七个金融类别，共涉及 4137 家金融机构和 32.87 万金融行业从业人员，本文后续相关结构分析亦是在此基础上作出的。互联网金融机构等未纳入本次统计调查和研究分析范围。

---

① 数据来源：市统计局《2018年上海统计年鉴》。

2017 年末上海金融行业从业人员状况

一、上海金融机构分布状况 ≫

　　为准确掌握上海金融机构的分布状况，本次调查对截至 2017 年末在上海注册的 4137 家金融机构进行统计分析。

（一）金融机构类别分布

　　按 7 大类分，金融机构数量由多到少依次为：地方金融机构 2562 家，证券业金融机构 927 家，保险业金融机构 364 家，银行业金融机构 240 家，银行卡清算、支付结算和征信机构 27 家，全国性金融市场和基础设施 15 家，国际金融组织 2 家（见图 1-1）。

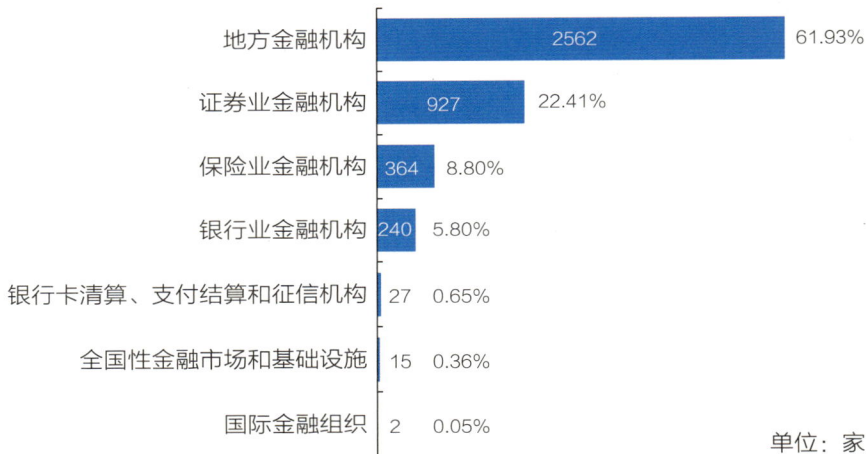

机构类别	数量	占比
地方金融机构	2562	61.93%
证券业金融机构	927	22.41%
保险业金融机构	364	8.80%
银行业金融机构	240	5.80%
银行卡清算、支付结算和征信机构	27	0.65%
全国性金融市场和基础设施	15	0.36%
国际金融组织	2	0.05%

单位：家

图 1-1　金融机构类别分布情况（按 7 大类分）

　　按 19 小类分，金融机构数量由多到少依次为：融资租赁公司 1891 家，证券公司 485 家，保险业金融机构 364 家，典当行 257 家，商业保理公司 247 家，私募基金管理人 188 家，银行业金融机构（银行类）171 家，期货公司 142 家，小额贷款公司 128 家，公募基金类企业 112 家，银行业金融机构（非银行）69 家，融资性担保公司 36 家，第三方支付机构 20 家，全国性金融市场和基础设施 15 家，银行卡清算机构 4 家，金融类征信机构 3 家，地方资产管理公司 2 家，国际金融组织 2 家，区域性股权市场 1 家（见图 1-2）。

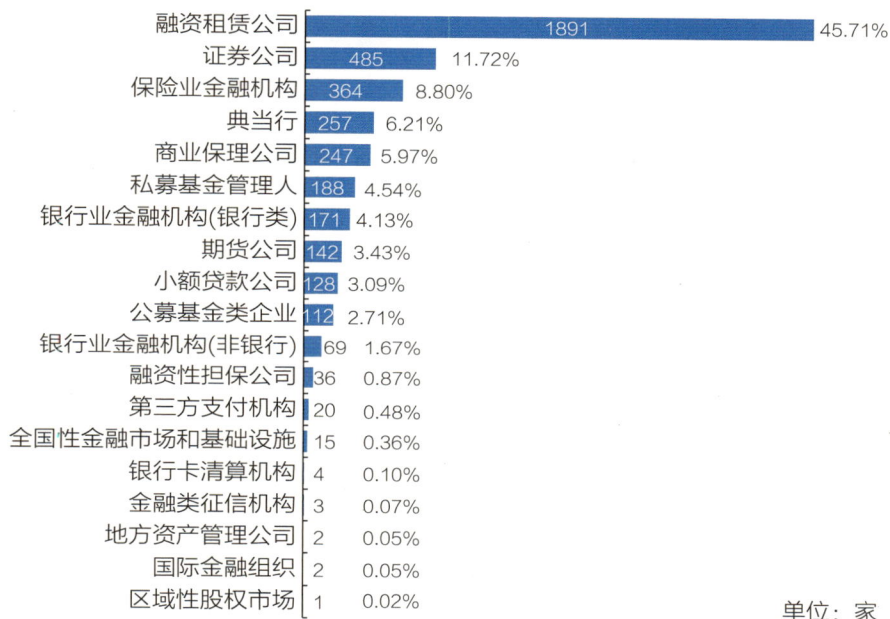

机构类别	数量	占比
融资租赁公司	1891	45.71%
证券公司	485	11.72%
保险业金融机构	364	8.80%
典当行	257	6.21%
商业保理公司	247	5.97%
私募基金管理人	188	4.54%
银行业金融机构(银行类)	171	4.13%
期货公司	142	3.43%
小额贷款公司	128	3.09%
公募基金类企业	112	2.71%
银行业金融机构(非银行)	69	1.67%
融资性担保公司	36	0.87%
第三方支付机构	20	0.48%
全国性金融市场和基础设施	15	0.36%
银行卡清算机构	4	0.10%
金融类征信机构	3	0.07%
地方资产管理公司	2	0.05%
国际金融组织	2	0.05%
区域性股权市场	1	0.02%

单位：家

图 1-2　金融机构类别分布情况（按 19 小类分）

（二）金融机构区域分布

按注册地划分，金融机构数量名列前五的分别是浦东新区、黄浦区、虹口区、静安区和徐汇区。其中，浦东新区 2744 家，总体占比 66.33%；黄浦区 235 家，总体占比 5.68%；虹口区 184 家，总体占比 4.45%；静安区 170 家，总体占比 4.11%；徐汇区 132 家，总体占比 3.19%；其余各区占比均在 3% 以下（见图 1-3）。

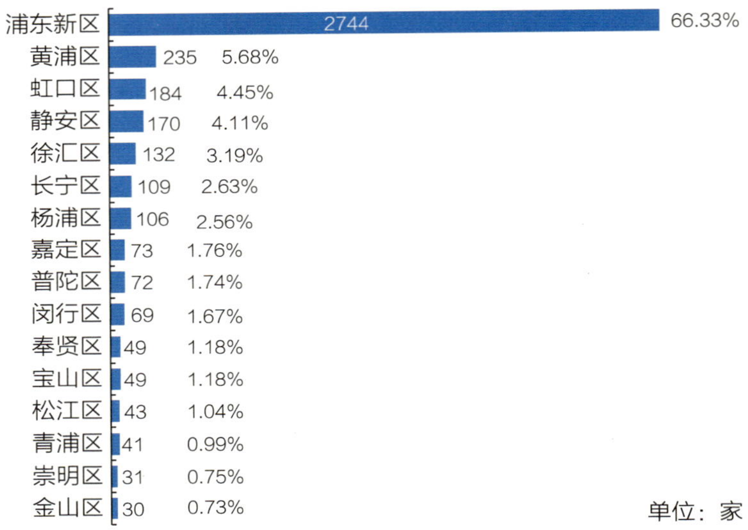

区域	数量	占比
浦东新区	2744	66.33%
黄浦区	235	5.68%
虹口区	184	4.45%
静安区	170	4.11%
徐汇区	132	3.19%
长宁区	109	2.63%
杨浦区	106	2.56%
嘉定区	73	1.76%
普陀区	72	1.74%
闵行区	69	1.67%
奉贤区	49	1.18%
宝山区	49	1.18%
松江区	43	1.04%
青浦区	41	0.99%
崇明区	31	0.75%
金山区	30	0.73%

单位：家

图 1-3 金融机构区域分布情况（按注册地划分）

二、上海金融行业从业人员总体状况 ≫

为准确掌握上海金融行业从业人员的总体状况，本次调查对统计范围内的 32.87 万从业人员进行了分析。

（一）人员总量

截至 2017 年末，纳入本次统计调查的上海金融行业从业人员总数为 328729 人。其中，男性 161955 人，占比 49.27%；女性 166774 人，占比 50.73%，男女比例大致均衡，女性从业人员数量略多于男性（见图 1-4）。

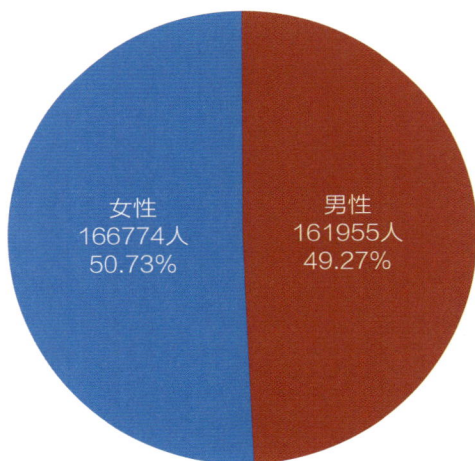

图 1-4　金融行业从业人员性别情况

从各区分布情况看，浦东新区人数最多，共 214330 人，占从业人员总数的 65.20%；黄浦区 61327 人，占 18.66%；静安区 16919 人，占 5.15%；虹口区 9360 人，占 2.85%；徐汇区 8902 人，占 2.71%；长宁区 5367 人，占 1.63%；其余各区占比均在 1% 以下（见图 1-5）。

浦东新区 ████████████████████████████████ 214330 65.20%
黄浦区 ███████ 61327 18.66%
静安区 ██ 16919 5.15%
虹口区 █ 9360 2.85%
徐汇区 █ 8902 2.71%
长宁区 █ 5367 1.63%
普陀区 | 2728 0.83%
杨浦区 | 2255 0.69%
金山区 | 1369 0.42%
闵行区 | 1355 0.41%
嘉定区 | 1314 0.40%
宝山区 | 984 0.30%
青浦区 | 718 0.22%
松江区 | 642 0.20%
奉贤区 | 616 0.19%
崇明区 | 543 0.17%

单位：人

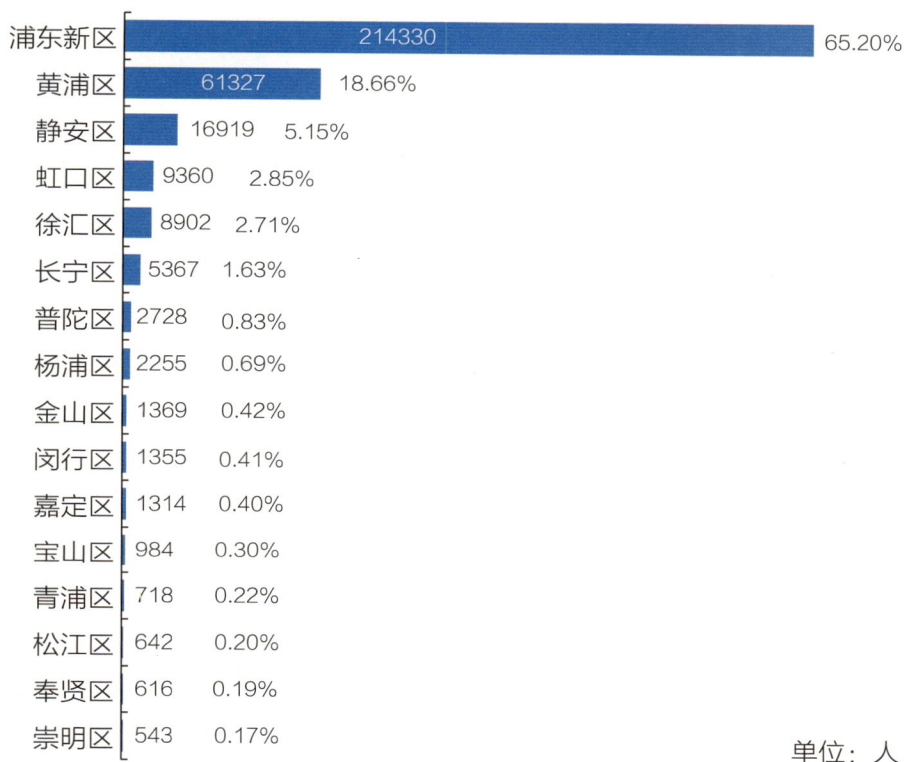

图 1-5　各区金融行业从业人员分布情况（按注册地划分）

（二）人员类型

从人员类型分布情况看，金融行业从业人员中在岗职工 280405 人，占从业人员总数的 85.30%；劳务派遣人员 22067 人，占从业人员总数的 6.71%；其他从业人员 26257 人，占从业人员总数的 7.99%（见图 1-6）。

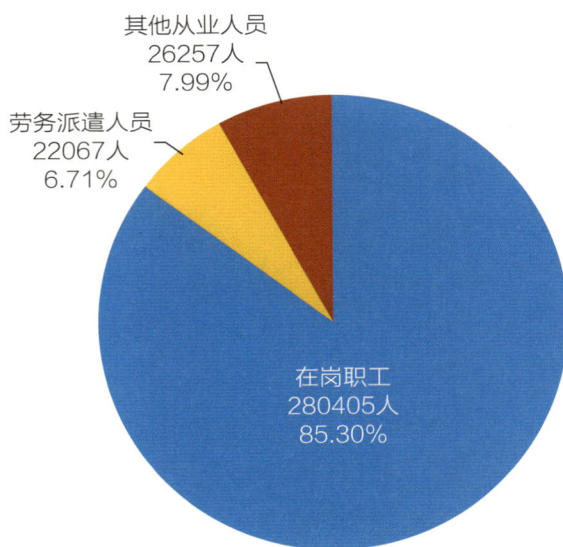

图 1-6　金融行业从业人员类型分布情况

　　按照惯例，港澳台和外籍金融从业人员统计在"其他从业人员"中。总体来看，港澳台和外籍人员数量不多，共 2163 人，其中 1141 人来自港澳台地区，1022 人为外籍人员（见图 1-7）。

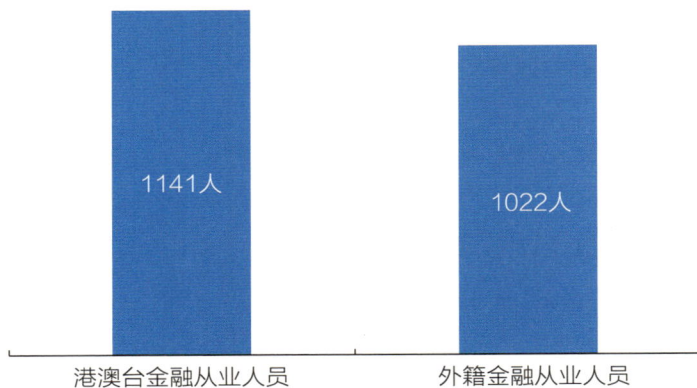

图 1-7　金融行业港澳台、外籍人员情况

（三）海外留学回国人员

在 328729 名金融从业人员中，海外留学回国人员有 25252 人，占从业人员总数的 7.68%（见图 1-8）。这包括由公派或自费出国（出境）学习，并获得国（境）外学士（含）以上学位的人员，或者在国（境）内获得大学本科（含）以上学历或中级（含）以上专业技术职务任职资格，并到国（境）外高等院校、科研机构进修一年（含）以上取得一定成果的访问学者或进修人员。

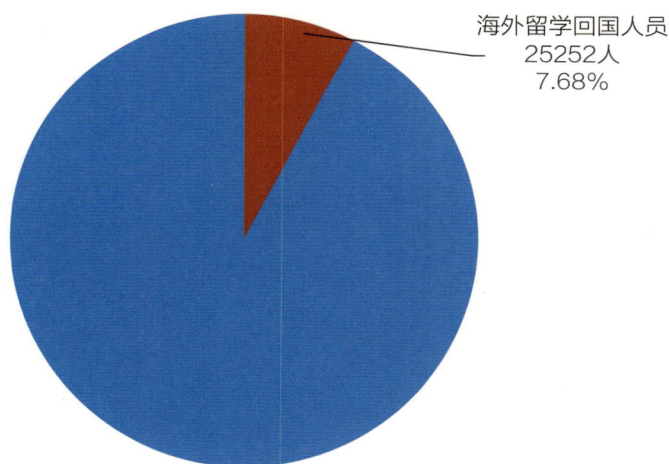

海外留学回国人员
25252人
7.68%

图 1-8　金融行业海外留学回国人员情况

（四）人员流动情况

2017 年全年，上海金融行业从业人员增加 73321 人，其中，海外招聘 1229 人，占人员增加总数的 1.68%；组织委派 537 人，占人员增加总数的 0.73%（见图 1-9）。

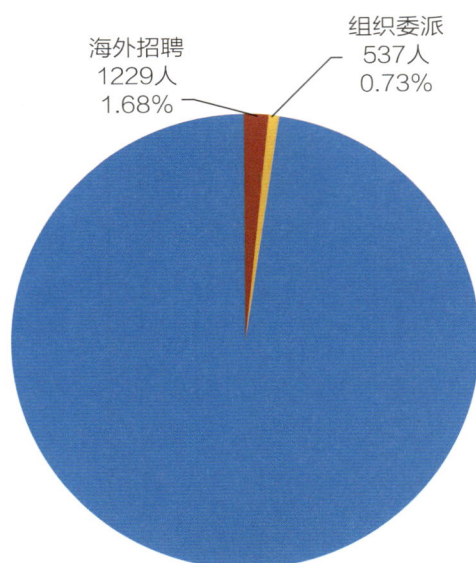

图 1-9   2017 年金融行业从业人员增加情况

2017 年全年，上海金融行业从业人员减少 66252 人，其中辞职人员 55020 人，占人员减少总数的 83.05%；辞退人员 5523 人，占人员减少总数的 8.34%（见图 1-10）。

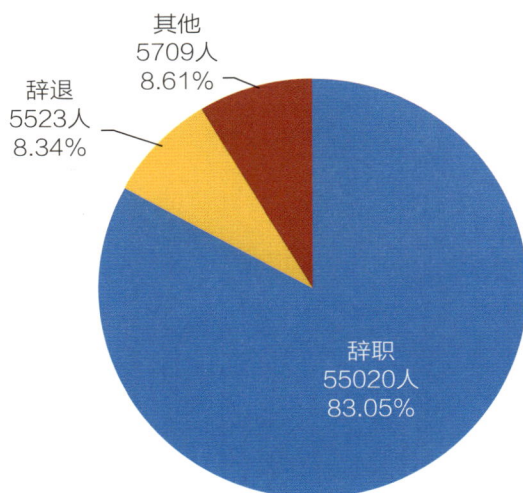

图 1-10   2017 年金融行业从业人员减少情况

三、上海金融行业从业人员结构状况 >>

截至 2017 年末，上海金融行业从业人员中的在岗职工人数为 280405 人。为更好地了解在岗职工结构状况，本次调查对在岗职工的年龄、文化程度、专业技术职称、职业水平认证等情况进行了统计分析。

（一）　年龄结构

从年龄结构看，在岗职工整体较为年轻。30 岁以下的人数占在岗职工总数的 34.84%；30 至 39 岁的占 42.39%；40 至 49 岁的占 16.63%；年龄在 50 岁以上的人数相对较少，其中 50 至 59 岁的占 5.80%（见图 1-11）。

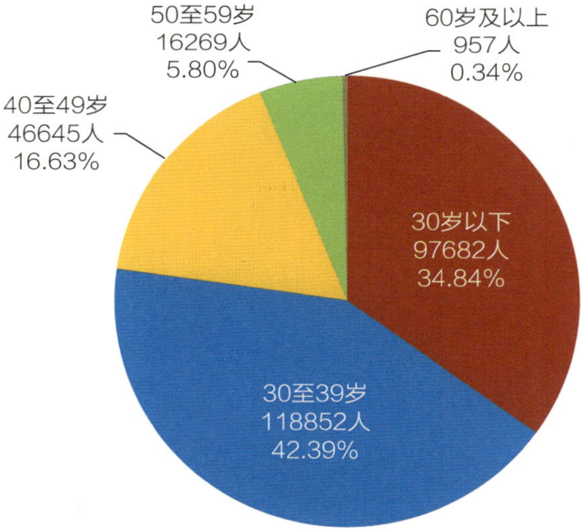

图 1-11　金融行业在岗职工年龄情况

（二）　学历结构

从学历结构看，83.44% 的在岗职工具有本科及以上学历，其中 58.25% 具有大学本科学历，24.35% 具有硕士研究生学历，0.84% 具有博士研究生学历。大专学历占 12.20%，中专、高中及以下占 4.36%（见图 1-12）。

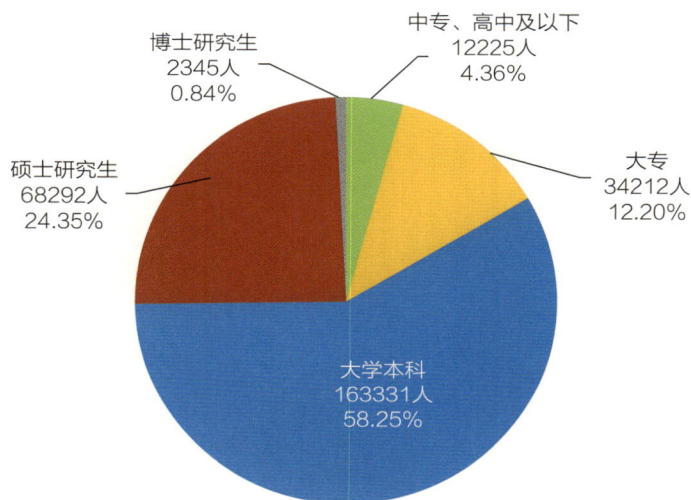

图 1-12　金融行业在岗职工学历情况

具有海外学历人员共 24421 人，占在岗职工总数的 8.71%。其中，具有海外大学本科学历的有 3796 人，占具有海外学历人员总数的 15.54%；具有海外硕士学历的有 20431 人，占 83.67%；具有海外博士学历的有 194 人，占 0.79%（见图 1-13）。

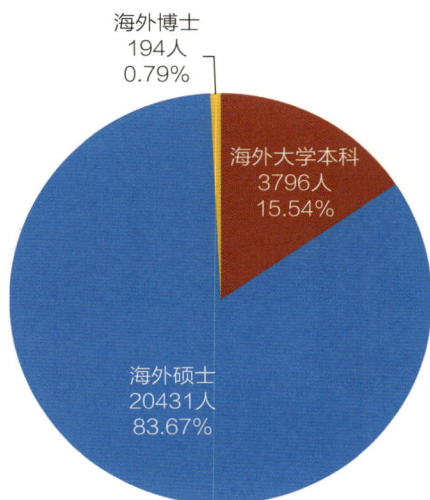

图 1-13　金融行业在岗职工具有海外学历人员情况

（三） 职称结构

从职称结构看，在岗职工中有 **22.50%** 获得专业技术职称。其中，具有中级专业技术职称的人员数量最多，为 **33689** 人，占在岗职工总数的 **12.01%**；具有初级专业技术职称的人数为 **26368** 人，占 **9.40%**；具有高级专业技术职称的人数为 **3058** 人，占 **1.09%**（见图 1-14）。

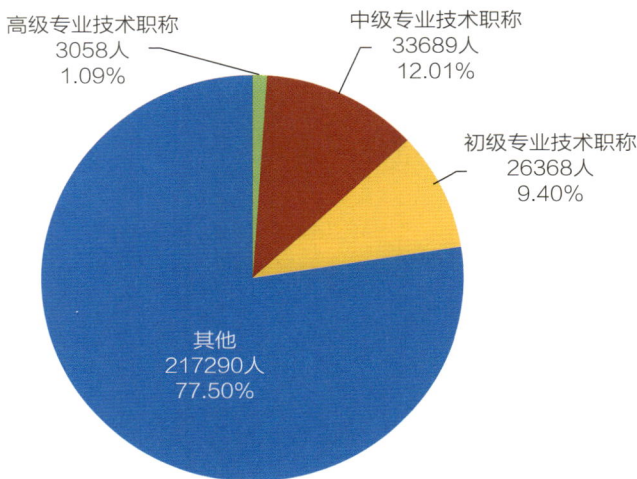

高级专业技术职称
3058人
1.09%

中级专业技术职称
33689人
12.01%

初级专业技术职称
26368人
9.40%

其他
217290人
77.50%

图 1-14 金融行业在岗职工专业技术职称情况

（四） 职业认证结构

从职业认证结构看，获得职业水平认证的在岗职工有 **19392** 人，占在岗职工总数的 **6.92%**。其中，获得国内职业水平认证的人数为 **12200** 人，占在岗职工总数的 **4.36%**，包括中国注册会计师、中国保险精算师、中国金融理财师等职业水平或职业能力认证项目。获得国外职业水平认证的人数为 **7192** 人，占在岗职工总数的 **2.56%**，包括英国精算师（IOA）、理财规划师（ChFP）、注册会计师（CPA）、金融理财师（AFP）、加拿大注册会计师（CGA）、金融风险管理师（FRM）、注册金融规划师（CFP）、国际注册内部审计师（CIA）、英国特许注册会计师（ACCA）、特许金融分析师（CFA）、北美精算师（SOA）、寿险管理师（LOMA）等（见图1-15）。

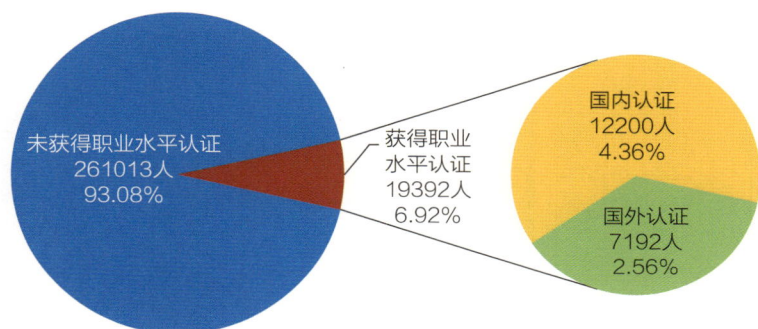

图 1-15　金融行业在岗职工获得职业水平认证情况

从获得职业准入资格的情况看，获得职业准入资格的在岗职工人数为85432人，占在岗职工总数的30.47%，包括银行、证券、保险等金融监管机构规定的从事金融工作必须要取得的行业准入资格（高管任职资格除外），如证券业从业人员资格、证券投资咨询人员从业资格、基金从业人员资格等（见图1-16）。

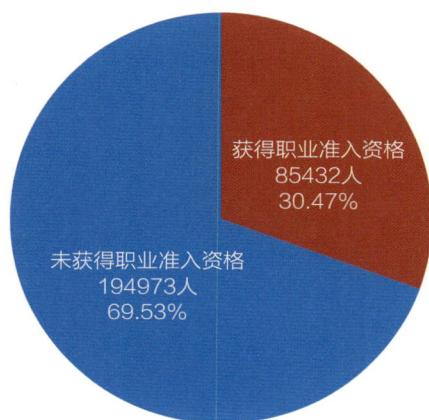

图 1-16　金融行业在岗职工获得职业准入资格情况

四、上海金融行业从业人员分布状况 ≫

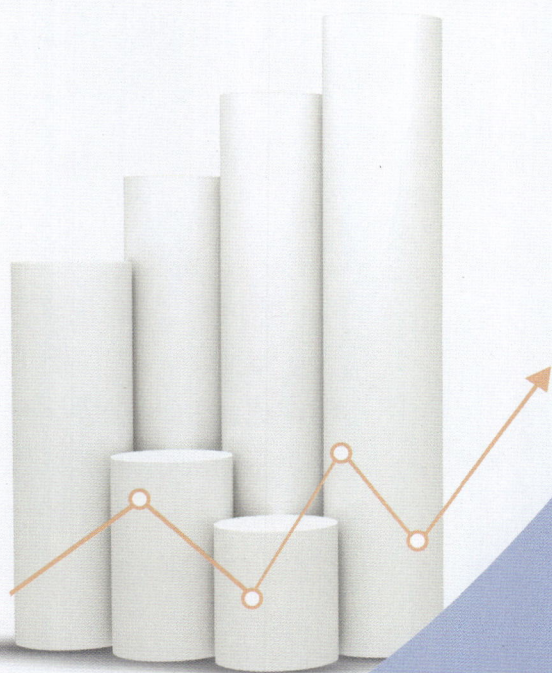

（一）各金融类别从业人员总体状况

为深入了解上海金融行业从业人员分布状况，本次调查对各金融类别的 32.87 万从业人员总体状况进行了分析。

1. 人员数量

按 7 大类分，银行业金融机构从业人员数为 153545 人，占从业人员总数的 46.71%；保险业金融机构从业人员数为 68998 人，占20.99%；证券业金融机构从业人员数为 61443 人，占 18.69%。总体来看，银行业、保险业以及证券业的从业人员数占比较高，共占从业人员总数的 86.39%（见图 1-17）。

银行业金融机构	153545	46.71%
保险业金融机构	68998	20.99%
证券业金融机构	61443	18.69%
地方金融机构	31104	9.46%
银行卡清算、支付结算和征信机构	10639	3.24%
全国性金融市场和基础设施	2898	0.88%
国际金融组织	102	0.03%

单位：人

图 1-17　各金融类别人员数量分布情况（按 7 大类分）

按 19 小类分，从业人员占比超过 10% 的有 3 个类别，其中银行业金融机构（银行类）从业人员数为 144137 人，占从业人员总数的 43.85%；保险业金融机构从业人员数为 68998 人，占 20.99%；证券公司从业人员数为 37832 人，占 11.51%。从业人员占比在 2% ～ 10% 之间的有 3 个类别，分别是融资租赁公司占 7.46%，公募基金类企业占 4.23%，银行业金融机构（非银行）占 2.86%。从

业人员占比在 1% ～ 2% 之间的有 4 个类别，分别是期货公司占
1.91%，第三方支付机构占 1.61%，银行卡清算机构占 1.59%，私募
基金管理人占 1.04%。从业人员占比在 1% 以下的有 9 个类别，分
别是全国性金融市场和基础设施占 0.88%，典当行占 0.74%，商业
保理公司占 0.53%，小额贷款公司占 0.51%，融资性担保公司占
0.14%，地方资产管理公司占 0.05%，金融类征信机构占 0.03%，国
际金融组织占 0.03%，区域性股权市场占 0.03%（见图 1-18）。

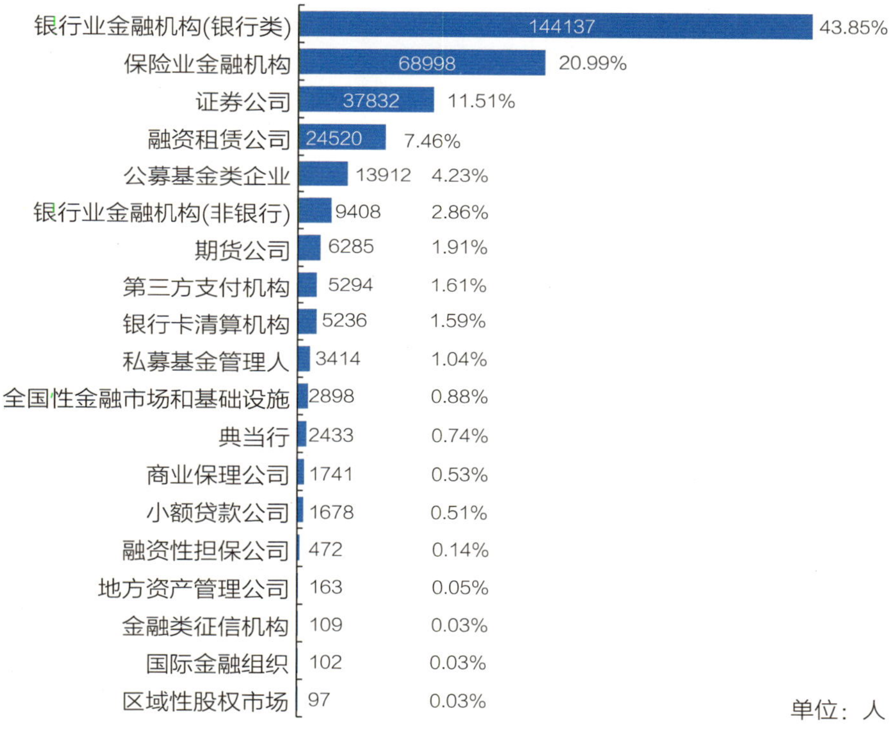

图 1-18 各金融类别人员数量分布情况（按 19 小类分）

2. 人员性别

从性别情况看，各金融类别中，银行业金融机构（银行类）和
区域性股权市场的女性从业人员多于男性，其中银行业金融机构
（银行类）女性 82689 人，占所在类别从业人员总数的 57.37%；区域
性股权市场女性 58 人，占所在类别从业人员总数的 59.79%。保险业

金融机构的女性从业人员占比为 **49.93%**，男女比例基本持平。证券公司、公募基金类企业、银行业金融机构（非银行）、期货公司、私募基金管理人、全国性金融市场和基础设施、典当行、小额贷款公司、商业保理公司、融资性担保公司、地方资产管理公司、金融类征信机构、国际金融组织等 14 个金融类别的女性从业人员占比均在 **40% ～ 49%** 之间，略低于男性。融资租赁公司、第三方支付机构和银行卡清算机构的女性从业人员占比在 **40%** 以下（见图 1-19）。

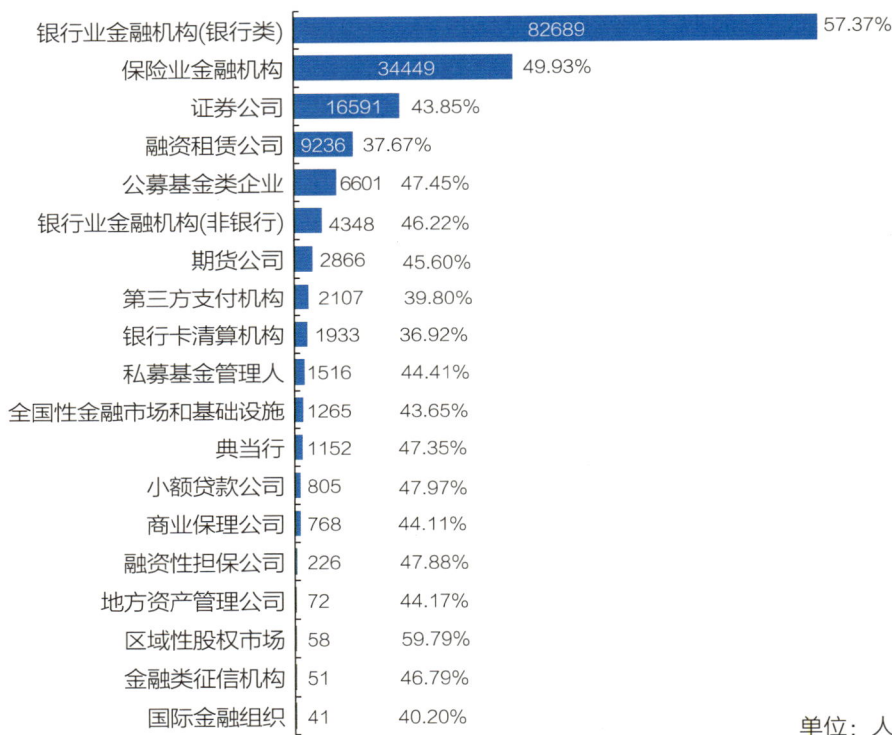

单位：人

图 1-19　各金融类别女性从业人员分布情况

3. 港澳台、外籍从业人员

统计数据显示，2163 名港澳台和外籍人员主要集中在银行业金融机构（银行类）、融资租赁公司和保险业金融机构，其中银行业金融机构（银行类）有 585 名外籍人员和 514 名港澳台人员，融资租赁公司有 41 名外籍人员和 272 名港澳台人员，保险业金融机构有

200 名外籍人员和 155 名港澳台人员。另外，在商业保理公司、证券公司、公募基金类企业、银行类金融机构（非银行）、期货公司、私募基金管理人和国际金融组织等 7 个金融类别也有少量的港澳台和外籍从业人员（见图 1-20）。

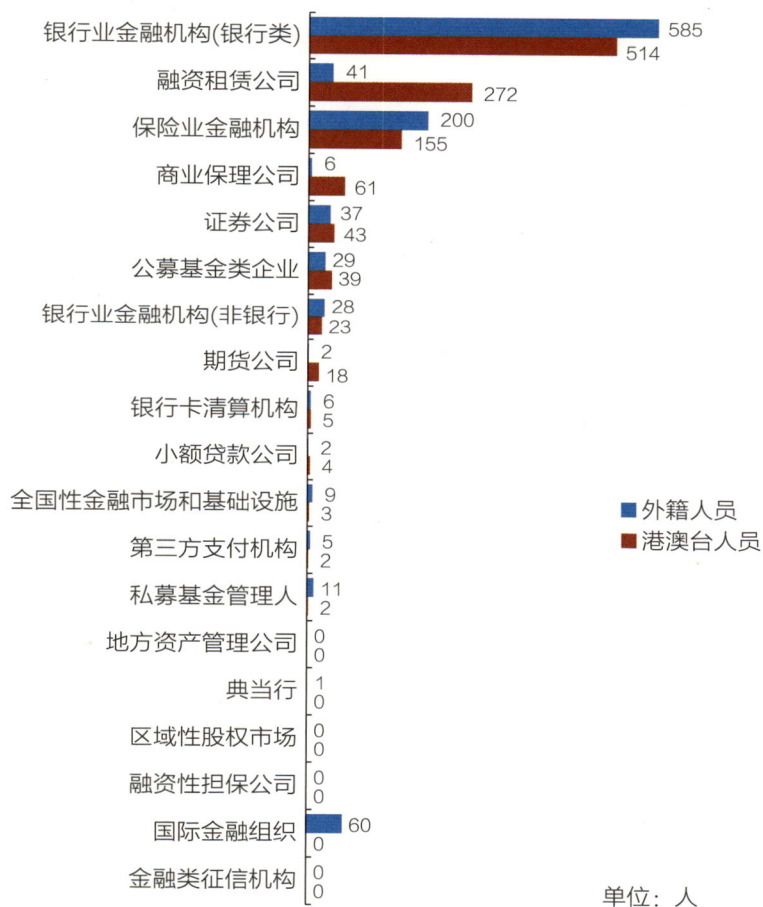

图 1-20　各金融类别港澳台、外籍人员分布情况

4. 人员流动情况

从人员流动情况看，2017 年全年人员增加数量居前四的依次是银行业金融机构（银行类）、保险业金融机构、融资租赁公司和证券公司。其中，银行业金融机构（银行类）增加 25496 人，保险业

金融机构增加 16332 人，融资租赁公司增加 9430 人，证券公司增加 9348 人。2017 年全年人员减少数量居前四的依次是银行业金融机构（银行类）、保险业金融机构、证券公司和融资租赁公司。其中，银行业金融机构（银行类）减少 25306 人，保险业金融机构减少 16073 人，证券公司减少 8410 人，融资租赁公司减少 5381 人。由此可见，银行业金融机构（银行类）、保险业金融机构、融资租赁公司和证券公司等 4 个金融类别的从业人员流动性较大。此外，公募基金类企业、银行业金融机构（非银行）、期货公司、私募基金管理人、第三方支付机构和银行卡清算机构等 6 个金融类别的从业人员具有一定程度的流动性，而全国性金融市场和基础设施、小额贷款公司、商业保理公司、典当行、国际金融组织、金融类征信机构、

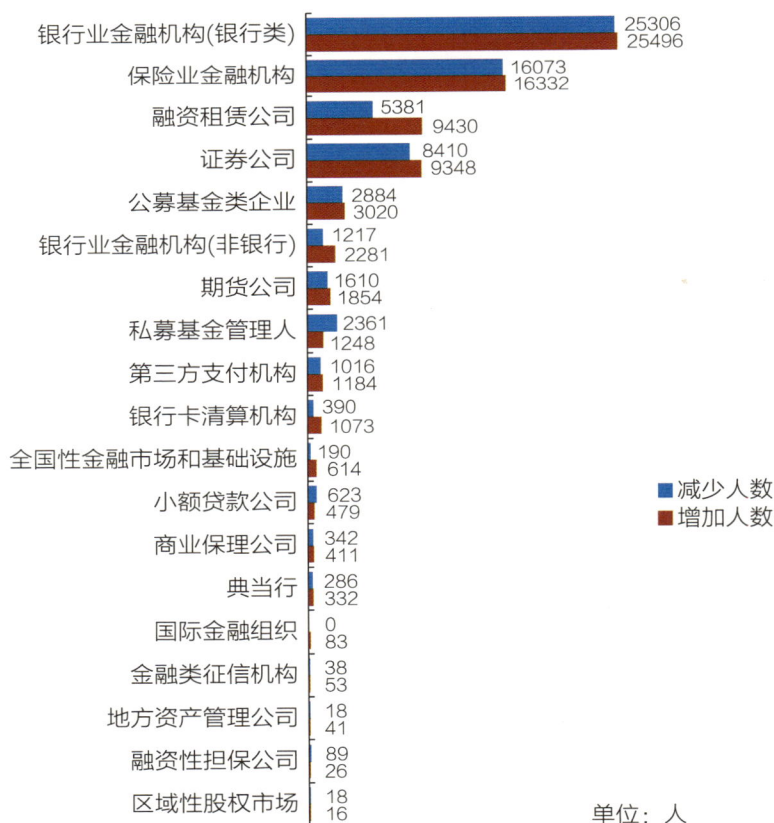

金融类别	减少人数	增加人数
银行业金融机构(银行类)	25306	25496
保险业金融机构	16073	16332
融资租赁公司	5381	9430
证券公司	8410	9348
公募基金类企业	2884	3020
银行业金融机构(非银行)	1217	2281
期货公司	1610	1854
私募基金管理人	2361	1248
第三方支付机构	1016	1184
银行卡清算机构	390	1073
全国性金融市场和基础设施	190	614
小额贷款公司	623	479
商业保理公司	342	411
典当行	286	332
国际金融组织	0	83
金融类征信机构	38	53
地方资产管理公司	18	41
融资性担保公司	89	26
区域性股权市场	18	16

■ 减少人数
■ 增加人数

单位：人

图 1-21　各金融类别人员流动情况

地方资产管理公司、融资性担保公司和区域性股权市场等 9 个金融类别的从业人员则相对稳定（见图 1-21）。

2017 年增加的人员中，通过海外招聘渠道增加人数较多的是银行业金融机构（银行类）、证券公司、保险业金融机构和国际金融组织等 4 个金融类别；第三方支付机构、区域性股权市场、融资租赁公司和私募基金管理人等 4 个金融类别的海外招聘人数较少。统计数据显示，通过组织委派安排任职的情况较多集中在银行业金融机构（银行类）、保险业金融机构和全国性金融市场和基础设施（见图 1-22）。

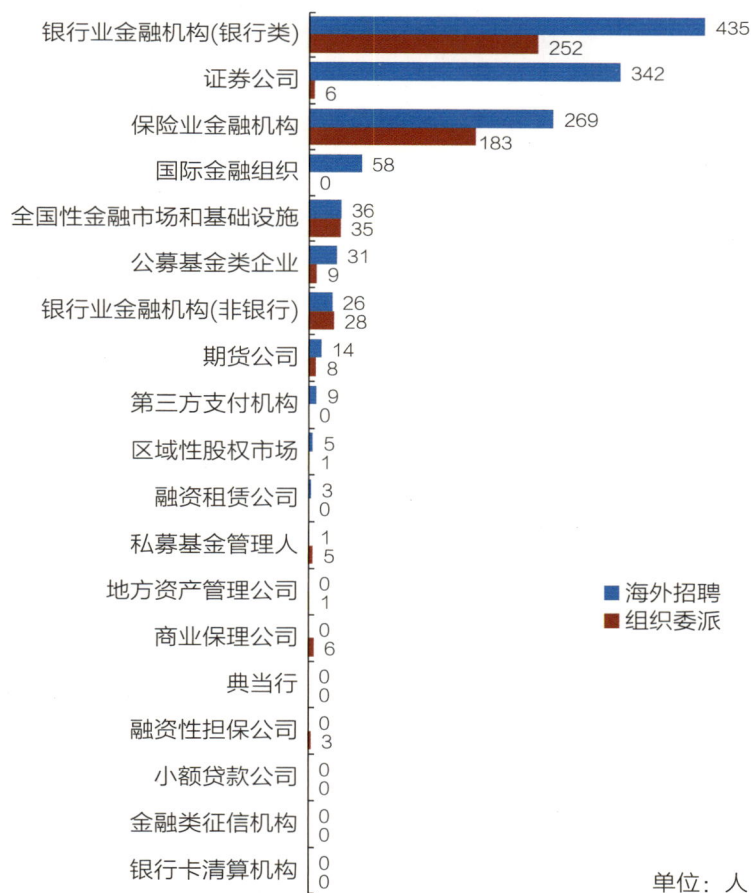

图 1-22　各金融类别从业人员海外招聘、组织委派分布情况

2017 年减少的人员中，辞职人数居前三的为银行业金融机构（银行类）、保险业金融机构和证券公司。其中 2017 年全年银行业金融机构（银行类）辞职人数为 21731 人，保险业金融机构辞职人数为 11837 人，证券公司辞职人数为 6177 人。融资性担保公司、金融类征信机构、区域性股权市场、地方资产管理公司和国际金融组织等 5 个金融类别的辞职人数较少。辞退人数较多的是保险业金融机构和证券公司，2017 年全年分别为 2147 人和 1996 人（见图 1-23）。

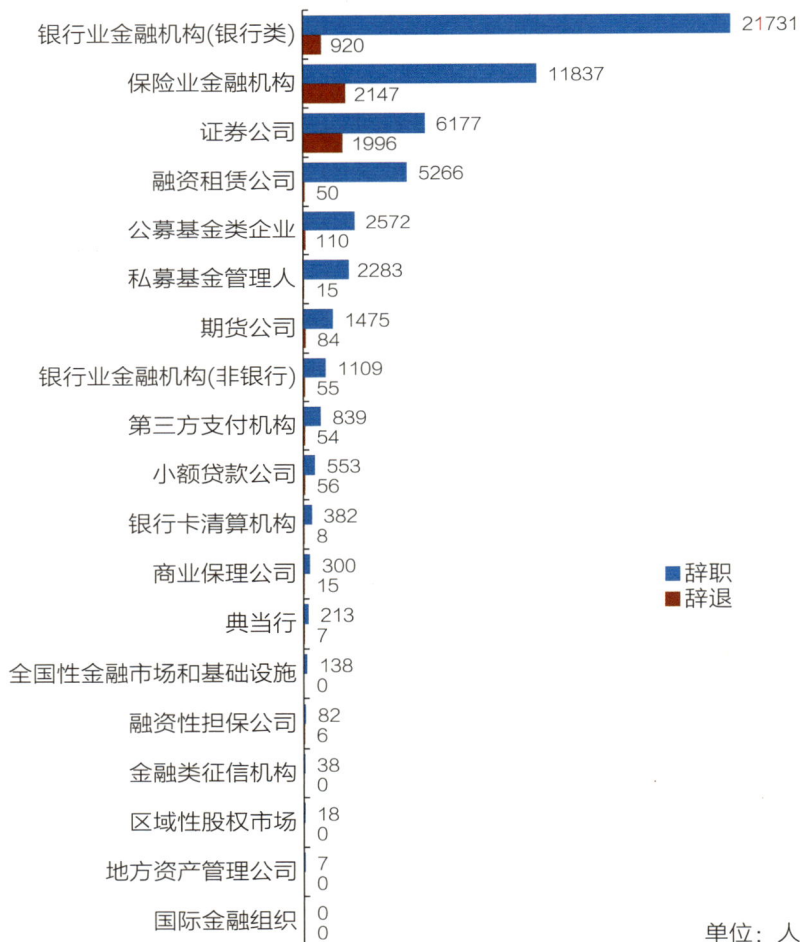

图 1-23　各金融类别从业人员辞职、辞退分布情况

（二）各金融类别从业人员结构状况

如前所述，截至 2017 年末，各金融类别共有在岗职工 280405 人，各金融类别的在岗职工在年龄结构、学历结构、职称结构、职业认证结构等方面具有不同的分布特点。

1. 年龄结构

从年龄结构看，年龄低于 39 岁的在岗职工占比超过 80% 的有 10 类，分别为第三方支付机构占 91.92%，商业保理公司占 91.46%，融资租赁公司占 89.45%，银行卡清算机构占 88.87%，银行业金融机构（非银行）占 86.54%，公募基金类企业占 86.52%，区域性股权市场占 84.95%，金融类征信机构占 81.65%，私募基金管理人占 81.26%，期货公司占 80.56%。年龄低于 39 岁的在岗职工占比在

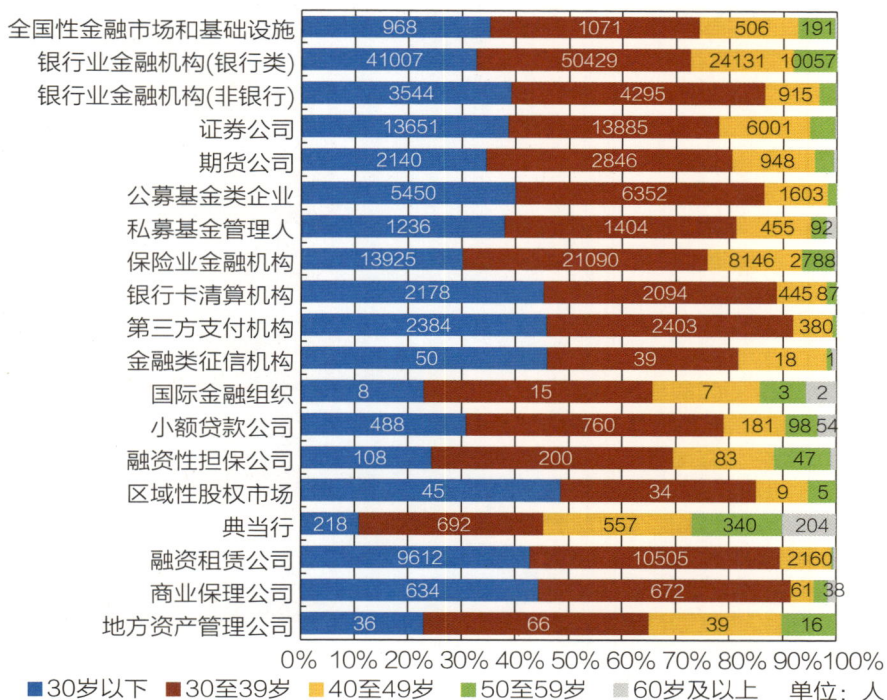

图 1-24　各金融类别在岗职工年龄结构分布情况

70% ～ 80% 之间的有 5 类，分别为小额贷款公司占 78.94%，证券公司占 77.98%，保险业金融机构占 75.86%，全国性金融市场和基础设施占 74.23%，银行业金融机构（银行类）占 72.75%。典当行、国际金融组织、融资性担保公司、地方资产管理公司的在岗职工年龄结构相对偏大，50 至 59 岁和 60 岁及以上的这两个年龄段人群占比较高，分别占比 27.05%、14.29%、11.74%、10.19%（见图 1-24）。

2.学历结构

各金融类别中，具有本科学历的在岗职工，商业保理公司占 71.64%，融资性担保公司占 67.95%，银行业金融机构（银行类）占 66.75%，期货公司占 62.38%，融资租赁公司占 60.95%，小额贷款公司占 57.18%，银行业金融机构（非银行）占 57.02%，保险业金融机构占 54.33%，第三方支付机构占 54.07%。具有硕士和博士研究生学

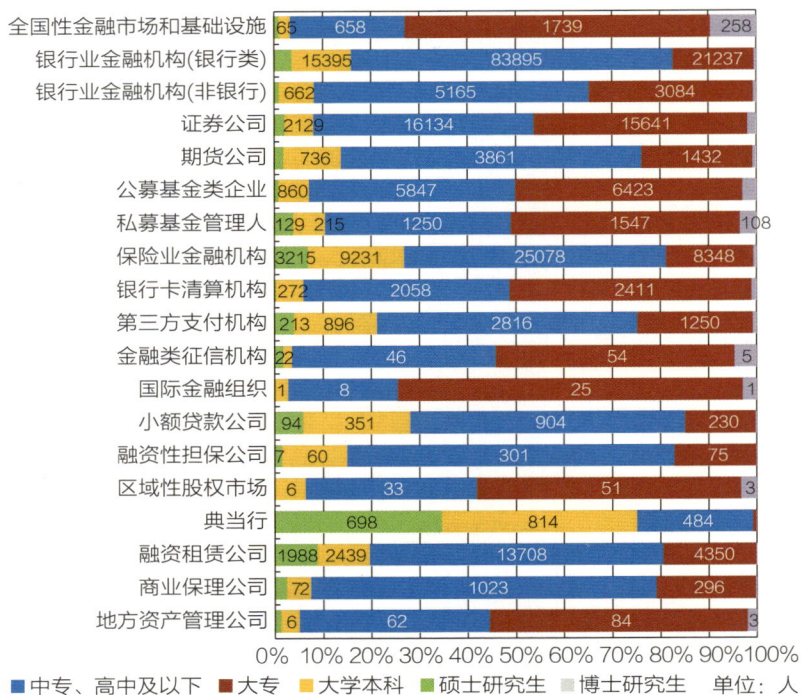

图 1-25　各金融类别在岗职工学历分布情况

历的在岗职工，国际金融组织分别占 73.53%、2.94%，全国性金融市场和基础设施分别占 63.31%、9.39%，区域性股权市场分别占 54.84%、3.23%，地方资产管理公司分别占 53.50%、1.91%，银行卡清算机构分别占 50.16%、0.98%。而大专学历，中专、高中及以下学历的人群主要集中在典当行、小额贷款公司、保险业金融机构和第三方支付机构，分别占 75.19%、28.15%、26.96%、21.29%（见图 1-25）。

从具有海外学历的人员情况看，各金融类别中，具有海外大学本科及以上学历的在岗职工人数分别为：银行业金融机构（银行类）7885 人，证券公司 5370 人，保险业金融机构 3112 人，公募基金类企业 2206 人，融资租赁公司 2032 人，银行业金融机构（非银行）1196 人，期货公司 623 人，私募基金管理人 595 人，银行卡清算机构 447 人，全国性金融市场和基础设施 421 人，第三方支付机构 214 人，小额贷款公司 149 人，商业保理公司 69 人，融资性担保公司 28 人，地方资产管理公司 21 人，区域性股权市场 21 人，金融类征信机构 19 人，典当行 11 人，国际金融组织 2 人（见图 1-26）。

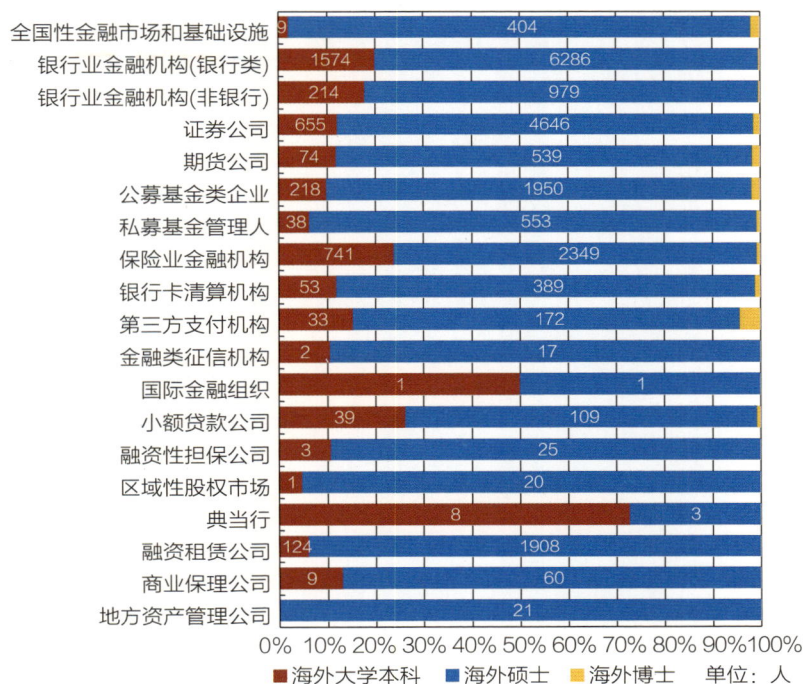

图 1-26　各金融类别在岗职工具有海外学历人员分布情况

3. 职称结构

从专业技术职称看，各金融类别中，银行业金融机构（非银行）和地方资产管理公司在岗职工具有专业技术职称的比例较高，分别占 37.40%、36.31%；商业保理公司、融资租赁公司、国际金融组织、第三方支付机构、保险业金融机构、私募基金管理人、公募基金类企业等 7 个金融类别有 90% 以上的在岗职工未获得专业技术职称（见图 1-27）。

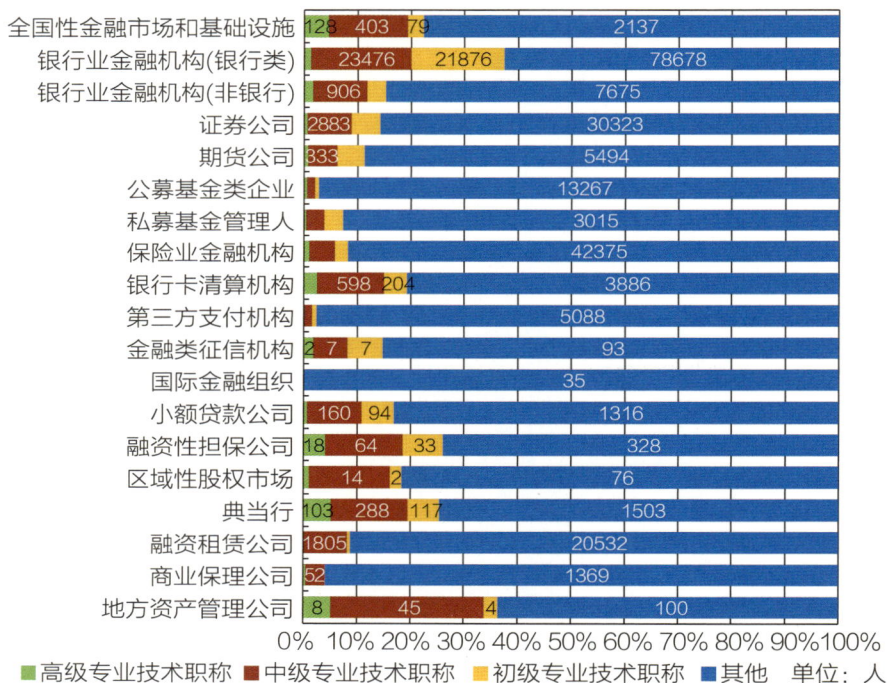

各金融类别在岗职工具有专业技术职称人员分布情况（图例：高级专业技术职称、中级专业技术职称、初级专业技术职称、其他 单位：人）

类别	高级	中级	初级	其他
全国性金融市场和基础设施	128	403	79	2137
银行业金融机构(银行类)		23476	21876	78678
银行业金融机构(非银行)		906		7675
证券公司		2883		30323
期货公司		333		5494
公募基金类企业				13267
私募基金管理人				3015
保险业金融机构				42375
银行卡清算机构		598	204	3886
第三方支付机构				5088
金融类征信机构	2	7	7	93
国际金融组织				35
小额贷款公司		160	94	1316
融资性担保公司	18	64	33	328
区域性股权市场		14	2	76
典当行	103	288	117	1503
融资租赁公司		1805		20532
商业保理公司		52		1369
地方资产管理公司	8	45	4	100

图 1-27　各金融类别在岗职工具有专业技术职称人员分布情况

总体来看，典当行和地方资产管理公司具有高级专业技术职称的在岗职工人数占所在类别在岗职工总数的比例较高，分别为 5.12% 和 5.10%。地方资产管理公司具有中级专业技术职称的在岗职工人数占比最高，为 28.66%。银行业金融机构（银行类）具有初级专业技术职称的在岗职工人数占比较高，为 17.40%。

4. 职业认证结构

在岗职工中获得职业水平认证的人员数量居前三的是银行业金融机构（银行类）、证券公司和保险业金融机构，分别有 8838 人、4012 人、3957 人，占各自所在类别在岗职工总数的 7.03%、11.36% 和 8.57%。典当行、融资租赁公司、银行卡清算机构和第三方支付机构获得职业水平认证人员占比较低，分别为 0.99%、0.82%、0.48% 和 0.42%（见图 1-28）。

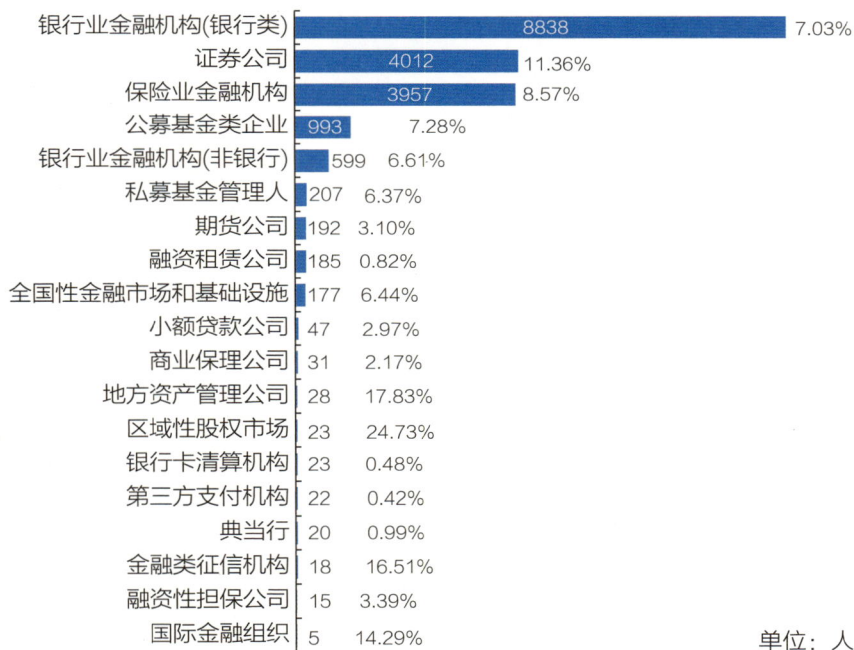

类别	人数	占比
银行业金融机构(银行类)	8838	7.03%
证券公司	4012	11.36%
保险业金融机构	3957	8.57%
公募基金类企业	993	7.28%
银行业金融机构(非银行)	599	6.61%
私募基金管理人	207	6.37%
期货公司	192	3.10%
融资租赁公司	185	0.82%
全国性金融市场和基础设施	177	6.44%
小额贷款公司	47	2.97%
商业保理公司	31	2.17%
地方资产管理公司	28	17.83%
区域性股权市场	23	24.73%
银行卡清算机构	23	0.48%
第三方支付机构	22	0.42%
典当行	20	0.99%
金融类征信机构	18	16.51%
融资性担保公司	15	3.39%
国际金融组织	5	14.29%

单位：人

图 1-28 各金融类别在岗职工获得职业水平认证人员分布情况

其中，在岗职工获得国外职业水平认证的人员数量居前三的是银行业金融机构（银行类）、保险业金融机构和证券公司，分别为 4794 人、829 人、717 人。而私募基金管理人、全国性金融市场和基础设施、期货公司、融资租赁公司、银行卡清算机构、金融类征信机构和地方资产管理公司等 7 个类别获得国外职业水平认证的人数相对较少。商业保理公司、小额贷款公司和第三方支付机构获得国外职业水平认证的人数相对更少。从占比上看,国际金融组织、金融类征信机构、地方资产管理公司获得国外职业水平认证的人数比例较高,分别占14.29%、11.01%、6.37%。期货公司、商业保理公司、银行卡清算机构、融资租赁公司、小额贷款公司、第三方支付机构获得国外职业水平认证的人数则分别占0.71%、0.56%、0.37%、0.12%、0.06%、0.02%(见图1-29)。

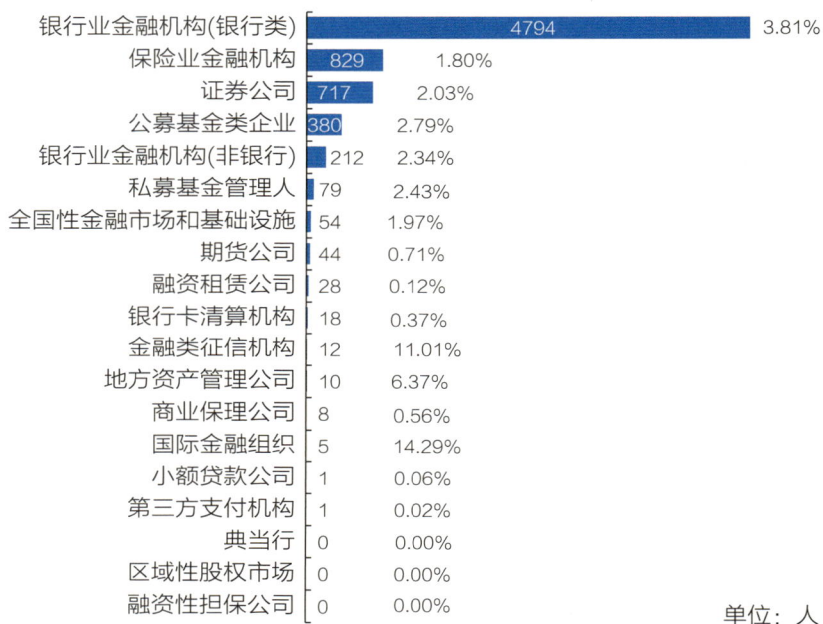

类别	人数	占比
银行业金融机构(银行类)	4794	3.81%
保险业金融机构	829	1.80%
证券公司	717	2.03%
公募基金类企业	380	2.79%
银行业金融机构(非银行)	212	2.34%
私募基金管理人	79	2.43%
全国性金融市场和基础设施	54	1.97%
期货公司	44	0.71%
融资租赁公司	28	0.12%
银行卡清算机构	18	0.37%
金融类征信机构	12	11.01%
地方资产管理公司	10	6.37%
商业保理公司	8	0.56%
国际金融组织	5	14.29%
小额贷款公司	1	0.06%
第三方支付机构	1	0.02%
典当行	0	0.00%
区域性股权市场	0	0.00%
融资性担保公司	0	0.00%

单位:人

图1-29 各金融类别在岗职工获得国外职业水平认证人员分布情况

INTRODUCTION

It is widely acknowledged that talent is essential for the making Shanghai as an international financial center. To generate a broad and accurate picture of the development and availability of financial talent in Shanghai, and to provide a basis for further research prior to formulating better policies to promote the development of financial institutions and attract financial professionals, CPC Shanghai Municipal Financial Work Committee, Shanghai Municipal Financial Service Office and Shanghai Municipal Statistics Bureau conducted the first joint survey of the financial services workforce in Shanghai in 2015, covering the employees of financial companies registered and engaging in financial service activities in Shanghai. The outcome document of the survey was entitled "Shanghai Financial Workforce Report 2015". The period from 2018 to 2020 is a critical stage in Shanghai's endeavor to complete the establishment of an international financial center based on the economic strength of China and the international status of RMB yuan. This new strategic goal poses new and higher demands for the development of financial professionals and talent base in Shanghai in terms of scale and expertise. To take stock of the availability and growth of financial talent in Shanghai, update statistics and realize well-informed decision-making to attract financial institutions and practitioners and build an international financial talent hub, CPC Shanghai Municipal Financial Work Committee, Shanghai Municipal Financial Services Bureau and Shanghai Municipal Statistics Bureau conducted a second joint survey of the financial services workforce in 2018, culminating in this new document "Shanghai Financial Services Workforce Statistics Report 2018".

I. Scope of survey

1. Financial institutions

The survey covers all institutions engaged in financial activities in Shanghai and registered before December 31, 2017. For the purpose of this survey, financial institutions are divided into seven categories: national financial markets and infrastructure; banking; securities; insurance; bank card clearing, settlement and credit reporting; international financial organizations; and local financial institutions.

Category 1: National financial markets and infrastructure

Shanghai Stock Exchange, Shanghai Futures Exchange, China Financial Futures Exchange, China Foreign Exchange Trading Center, Shanghai Gold Exchange, Shanghai Insurance Exchange, Shanghai Commercial Paper Exchange Corporation, Shanghai Clearing House, China Trust Registration Company Limited, CSDC Shanghai, and CIPS Shanghai, etc.

Category 2: Banking institutions

(1) Banks, including policy banks, state-owned banks, joint-stock commercial banks, city commercial banks, rural commercial banks, rural

banks, foreign banks, private banks, licensed banking centers (for funds, notes, private banking, precious metals, RMB trading, credit card, and financial services for small businesses), regional headquarters of banks in Shanghai, as well as financial technology companies (including data centers and software centers);

(2) Non-banks, including trust companies, currency brokerage companies, consumer finance companies, financial leasing companies, group finance companies, auto finance companies, financial assets & investment companies.

Category 3: Securities institutions

(1) Securities companies, including securities companies registered in Shanghai, Shanghai branches or business units of securities companies registered elsewhere, securities & investment consulting companies, underwriting and sponsor arms of securities companies, securities dealers, and securities-based asset management companies;

(2) Futures, including futures companies registered in Shanghai, Shanghai branches or business units of futures companies registered elsewhere;

(3) Public funds, including fund companies (public offerings), subsidiaries of fund companies, fund sales agencies;

(4) Private equity fund managers, including managers of private equity funds (including QFLPs), private securities funds, and other funds (including QDLPs) with an asset size of over RMB 1 billion.

Category 4: Insurance institutions

Insurance groups, life insurance companies, property insurance companies, reinsurance companies, pension companies, health insurance companies, agricultural insurance companies, regional headquarters of insurance companies in Shanghai, insurance brokers and agencies, insurance appraisal companies, shipping insurance centers, insurance-based asset management companies, and captive insurance companies, etc.

Category 5: Bank card clearing, settlement and credit reporting institutions

(1) Bank card clearing agencies;

(2) Third-party payment agencies;

(3) Financial credit reporting agencies.

Category 6: International financial organizations

New Development Bank and CCP12.

Category 7: Local financial organizations

(1) Micro-loan companies;

(2) Financing guarantee companies;

(3) Regional equity markets;

(4) Pawnshops;

(5) Financial leasing companies;

(6) Commercial factoring companies;

(7) Local asset management companies.

2. Workforce

For the purpose of this survey, the term "financial services workforce" refers to financial professionals who are working for the above-mentioned financial institutions and are directly remunerated for the services they render to, or otherwise benefiting from the operating income of, the said institutions as of December 31, 2017. The financial services workforce includes employees, leased staff and other practitioners, but excludes those who have left but still keep the employment relation and regularly receive basic allowances; students on interns; employees already recruited by PLA; and employees of external contractors.

II. Survey method

This survey includes a major survey and a supplementary sampling survey. The major survey embraces financial institutions hiring over 100 professionals while the sampling survey covers financial institutions having fewer than 100 practitioners.

III. Survey content

The survey aims to collect: first, basic information of financial institutions, including institution names, operating addresses and address codes, registered addresses and address codes, zip codes and industry segmentation; second, basic information of the workforce, including the size at the end of the year, practitioners' age, education background, professional accreditation, occupational qualification, and the mobility of workforce.

IV. Special notes

As of the end of 2017, the financial industry in Shanghai had 355,400 practitioners[1]. The survey and analysis focus on the seven major categories of the financial industry, covering 4,137 institutions and 328,700 individual practitioners. The survey and the subsequent analysis don't include Internet-based financial institutions.

---

[1] Source: Shanghai Municipal Statistics Bureau, 2018 Shanghai Statistical Yearbook.

FINANCIAL SERVICES WORKFORCE IN SHANGHAI AS OF THE END OF 2017

I. Overview of financial institutions in Shanghai

This report surveys 4,137 financial institutions registered in Shanghai as of the end of 2017.

1 Classification

Financial institutions in Shanghai are divided into 7 categories: local financial institutions (2,562), securities institutions (927), insurance institutions (364), banking institutions (240), bank card clearing, settlement and credit reporting agencies (27), national financial markets and infrastructure (15), and international financial organizations (2) (see Figure 1-1).

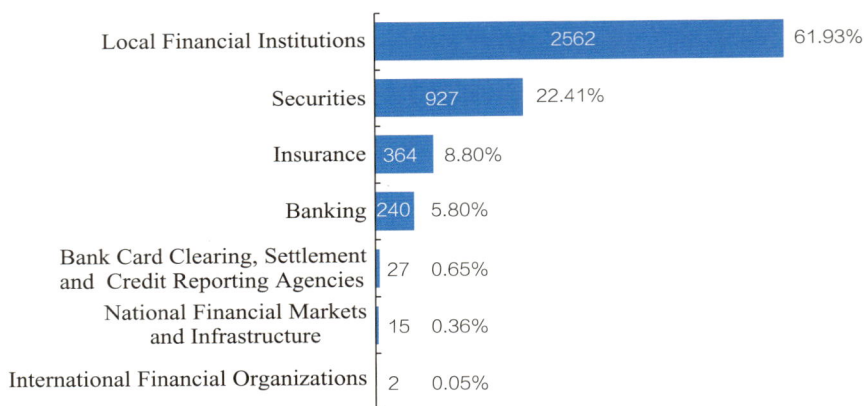

Local Financial Institutions	2562 — 61.93%
Securities	927 — 22.41%
Insurance	364 — 8.80%
Banking	240 — 5.80%
Bank Card Clearing, Settlement and Credit Reporting Agencies	27 — 0.65%
National Financial Markets and Infrastructure	15 — 0.36%
International Financial Organizations	2 — 0.05%

Figure 1-1   Seven categories of financial institutions

Financial institutions in Shanghai are further divided into 19 sub-categories: financial leasing companies (1,891), securities companies (485), insurance financial institutions (364), pawnshops (257), commercial factoring companies (247), private equity fund managers (188), banking institutions (banks) (171), futures companies (142), micro-loan companies (128), public fund managers (112), banking institutions (non-banks) (69), financing guarantee companies (36), third-party payment institutions (20), national financial markets and infrastructure (15), bank card clearing agencies (4), credit reporting agencies (3), local asset management companies (2), international financial organizations (2) and regional equity markets (1) (see Figure 1-2).

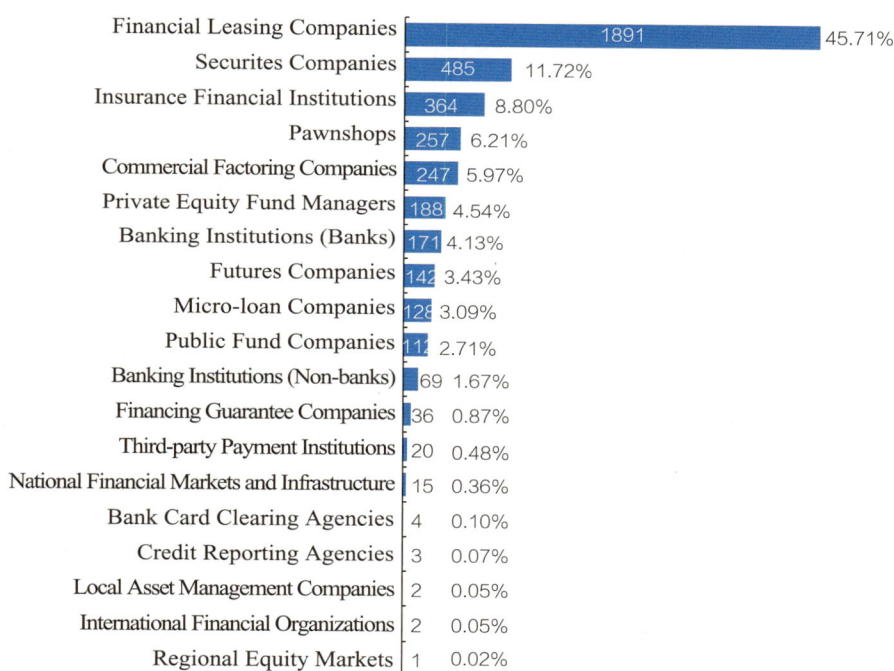

Category	Count	Percent
Financial Leasing Companies	1891	45.71%
Securites Companies	485	11.72%
Insurance Financial Institutions	364	8.80%
Pawnshops	257	6.21%
Commercial Factoring Companies	247	5.97%
Private Equity Fund Managers	188	4.54%
Banking Institutions (Banks)	171	4.13%
Futures Companies	142	3.43%
Micro-loan Companies	128	3.09%
Public Fund Companies	112	2.71%
Banking Institutions (Non-banks)	69	1.67%
Financing Guarantee Companies	36	0.87%
Third-party Payment Institutions	20	0.48%
National Financial Markets and Infrastructure	15	0.36%
Bank Card Clearing Agencies	4	0.10%
Credit Reporting Agencies	3	0.07%
Local Asset Management Companies	2	0.05%
International Financial Organizations	2	0.05%
Regional Equity Markets	1	0.02%

Figure 1-2   Nineteen sub-categories of financial institutions

2 Locational distribution

By the number of locally registered financial institutions, the top five districts are Pudong New Area (2,744, or 66.33%), Huangpu District (235, or 5.68%), Hongkou District (184, or 4.45%), Jing'an District (170, or 4.11%) and Xuhui District (132, or 3.19%). No other district in Shanghai has more than 3% (see Figure 1-3).

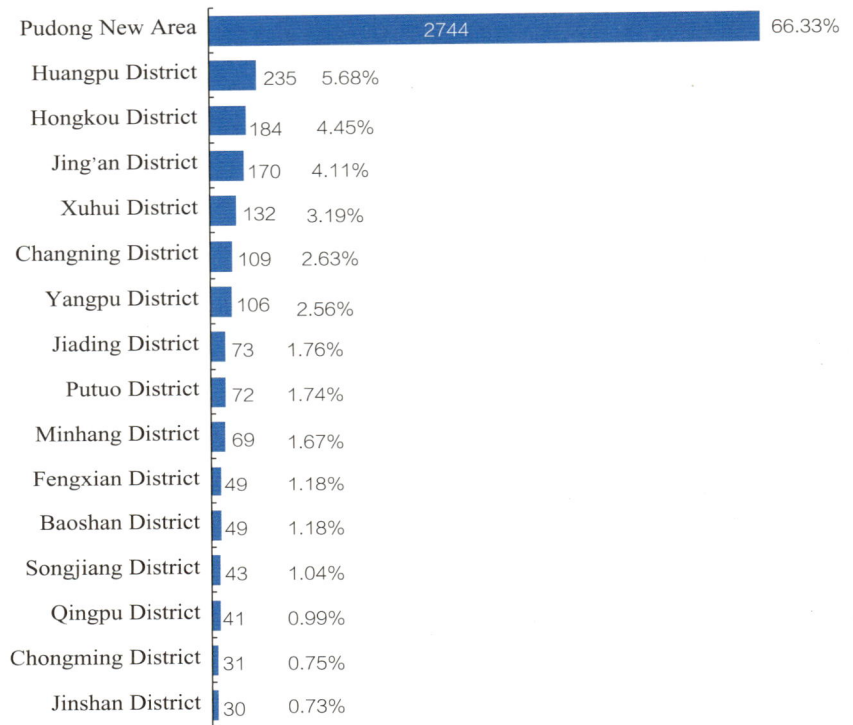

District	Count	Percentage
Pudong New Area	2744	66.33%
Huangpu District	235	5.68%
Hongkou District	184	4.45%
Jing'an District	170	4.11%
Xuhui District	132	3.19%
Changning District	109	2.63%
Yangpu District	106	2.56%
Jiading District	73	1.76%
Putuo District	72	1.74%
Minhang District	69	1.67%
Fengxian District	49	1.18%
Baoshan District	49	1.18%
Songjiang District	43	1.04%
Qingpu District	41	0.99%
Chongming District	31	0.75%
Jinshan District	30	0.73%

Figure 1-3 Locational distribution of financial institutions (by registration)

II. Overview of the financial services workforce in Shanghai

To create a more accurate and meaningful picture of all financial personnel in Shanghai, we analyzed all the 328,729 practitioners covered in our survey.

1 Size and classification

As of the end of 2017, there were 328,729 financial practitioners in Shanghai who are all covered in this survey. Among them, 161,955 (49.27%) are male; 166,774 (50.73%) are female (see Figure 1-4).

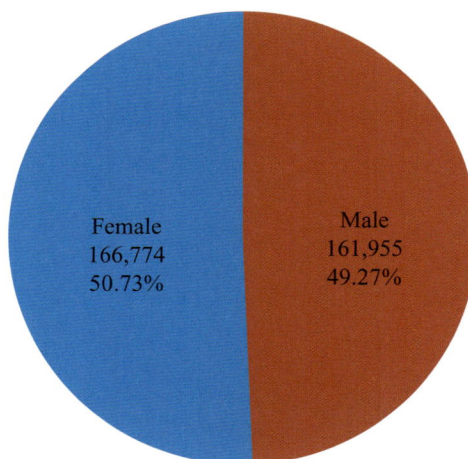

Female
166,774
50.73%

Male
161,955
49.27%

Figure 1-4　Gender mix of the financial services workforce

In terms of the locational distribution, Pudong New Area has the largest workforce (214,330 practitioners, or 65.20%); Huangpu District has 61,327 (18.66%); Jing'an District has 16,919 (5.15%); Hongkou District has 9,360 (2.85%); Xuhui District has 8,902 (2.71%); Changning District has 5,367 (1.63%); the rest has less than 1% (see Figure 1-5).

District	Value	Percent
Pudong New Area	214330	65.20%
Huangpu District	61327	18.66%
Jing'an District	16919	5.15%
Hongkou District	9360	2.85%
Xuhui District	8902	2.71%
Changning District	5367	1.63%
Putuo District	2728	0.83%
Yangpu District	2255	0.69%
Jinshan District	1369	0.42%
Minhang District	1355	0.41%
Jiading District	1314	0.40%
Baoshan District	984	0.30%
Qingpu District	718	0.22%
Songjiang District	642	0.20%
Fengxian District	616	0.19%
Chongming District	543	0.17%

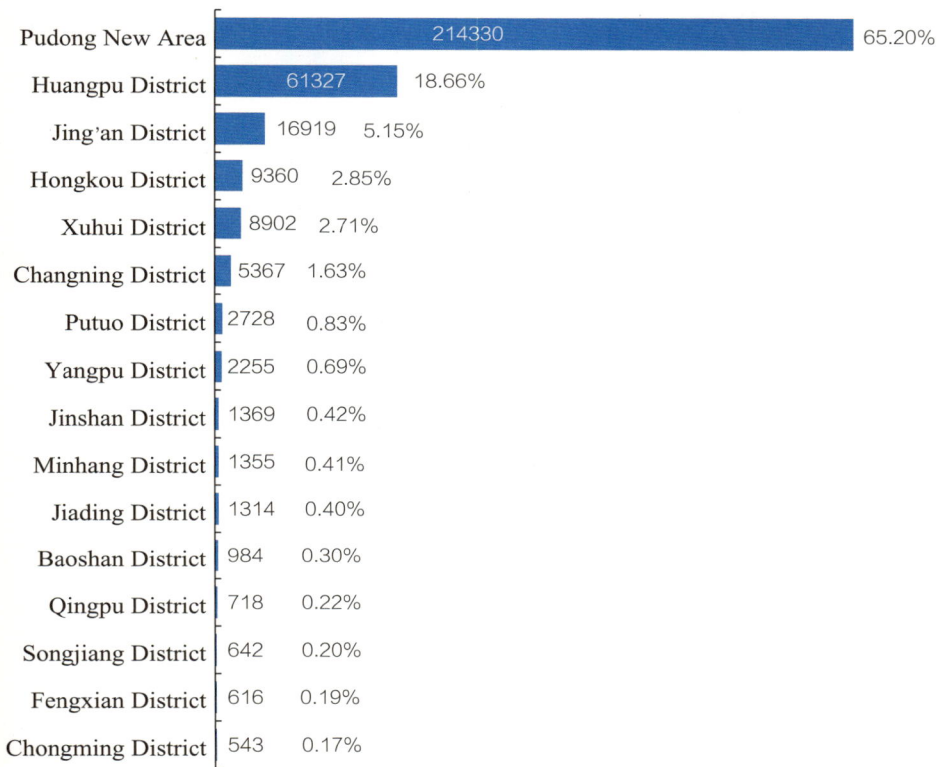

Figure 1-5   Spatial distribution of the financial services workforce (by registration)

2 Employment of the workforce

By the classification, the financial services workforce of Shanghai includes 280,405 employees (85.30%); 22,067 leased staff (6.71%); 26,257 other practitioners (7.99%) (see Figure 1-6).

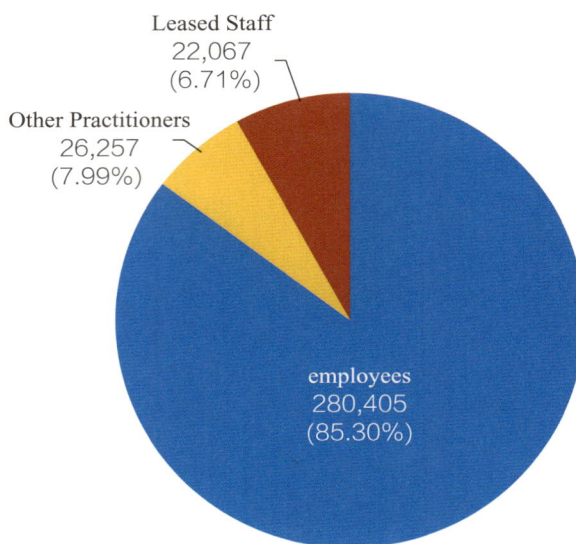

Figure 1-6   Classification of the financial services workforce

Following the usual practices, financial practitioners from Hong Kong, Macao and Taiwan and foreign countries are recorded under "Other Practitioners". Overall, the number of practitioners from Hong Kong, Macao, Taiwan and foreign countries is small, a total of 2,163 people, in which 1,141 are from Hong Kong, Macao and Taiwan, and 1,022 are foreigners (see Figure 1-7).

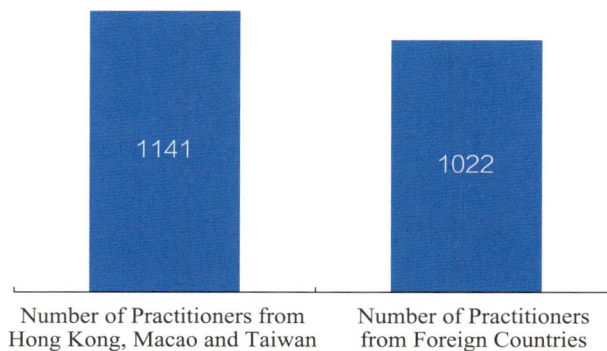

Figure 1-7   Financial practitioners from Hong Kong, Macao, Taiwan and foreign countries

③ Returnees from overseas studies

The financial services workforce of Shanghai includes 25,252 (7.68%) returnees from overseas studies (see Figure 1-8), including: people who have studied abroad with public funding or at their own expense and got a Bachelor's or advanced degree; those who have already obtained a Bachelor's or advanced degree and/or intermediate or higher professional qualifications in China, and have further studied overseas as visiting scholars or research fellows for a year or more.

Financial Services
Workforce of Shanghai
25,252
(7.68%)

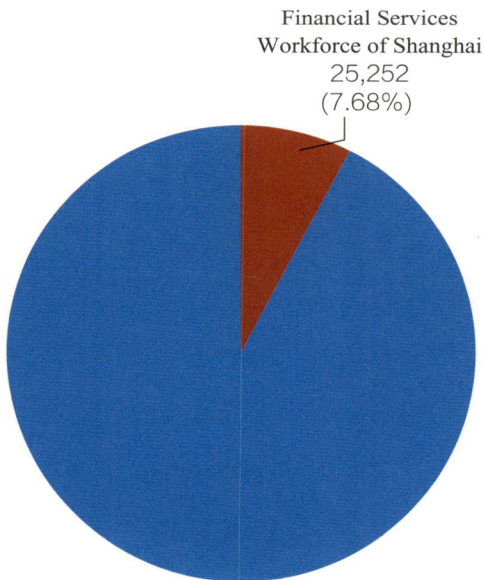

Figure 1-8   Financial practitioners returning from overseas studies

④ Workforce mobility

The year 2017 saw an inflow of 73,321 new financial practitioners in Shanghai, in which 1,229 (1.68%) were recruited overseas and 537 (0.73%) were assigned to Shanghai from headquarters (see Figure 1-9).

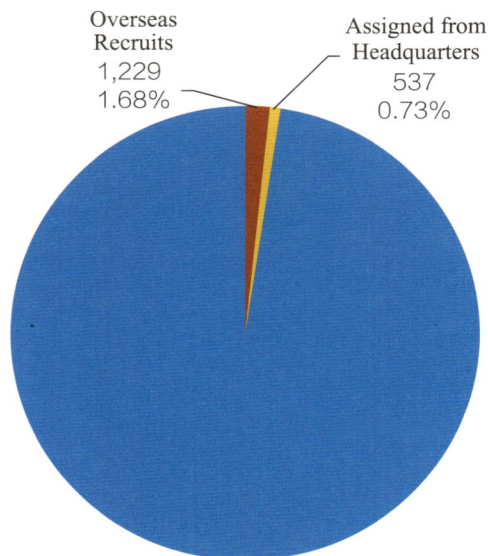

Figure 1-9   Inflow of financial practitioners in 2017

The same year also witnessed the departure of 66,252 financial practitioners in Shanghai, in which 55,020 (83.05%) resigned and 5,523 8.34% were dismissed (see Figure 1-10).

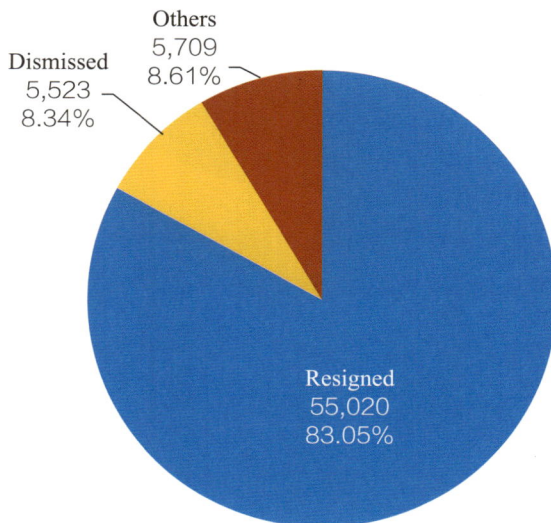

Figure 1-10   Departure of financial practitioners in 2017

III. Composition of employees of financial institutions in Shanghai

As of the end of 2017, the financial services workforce in Shanghai included 280,405 employees. To generate a better view of the financial employees in Shanghai, the survey classifies the employees of financial institutions by age, academic background, professional qualification and accreditation.

1 Age profile

From the perspective of age group, the financial employees are relatively young overall. 34.84% of the employees are under 30; 42.39% between 30 and 39; 16.63% between 40 and 49; the share of people over 50 is relatively small, with 5.80% aged from 50 to 59 (see Figure 1-11).

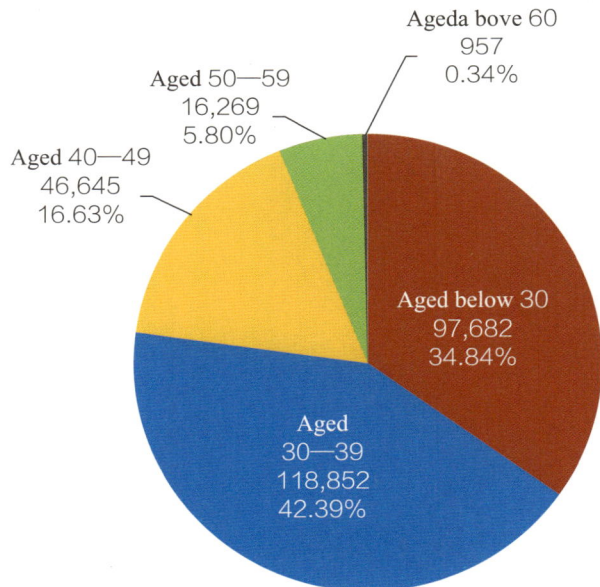

Figure 1-11   Age profile of employees of financial institutions in Shanghai

2 Education background

83.44% of the employees of financial institutions in Shanghai have a Bachelor's or advanced degree: 58.25% have a Bachelor's degree, 24.35% have a Master's degree, and 0.84% have a doctoral degree. Those with a higher vocational degree account for 12.20%, and those with secondary vocational, high school and even lower diplomas have a slim combined share of 4.36% (see Figure 1-12).

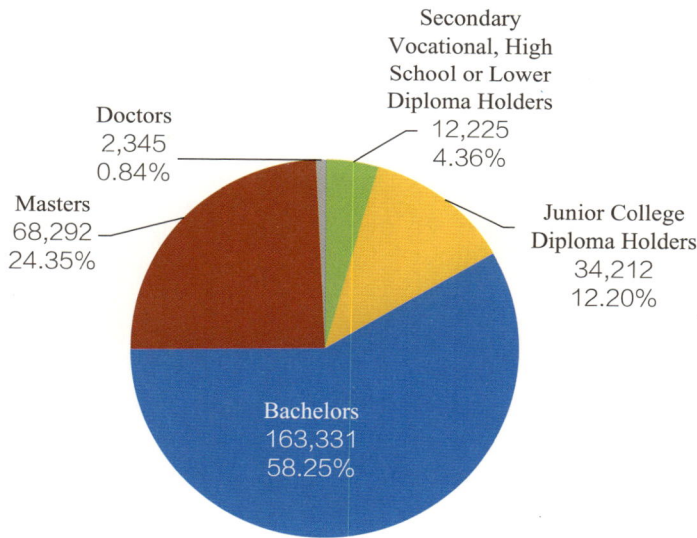

Figure 1-12   Education background of employees of financial institutions in Shanghai

24,421 (8.71%) financial employees have overseas education background. Among them, 3,796 (15.54%) have won a Bachelor's degree overseas; 20,431 (83.67%) have a Master's degree; and 194 (0.79%) have a doctoral degree (see Figure 1-13).

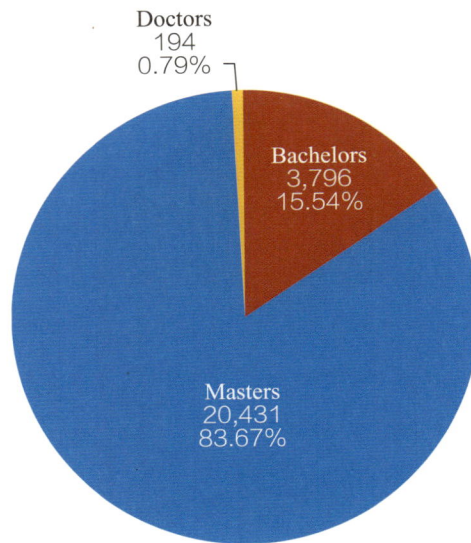

*Figure 1-13   Employees with overseas education background
in financial institutions in Shanghai*

3 Professional qualifications

22.50% of the employees of financial institutions in Shanghai have professional titles. Among them, 33,689 (12.01%) have an intermediate professional title; 26,368 (9.40%) have a junior title; and 3,058 (1.09%) have a senior title (see Figure 1-14).

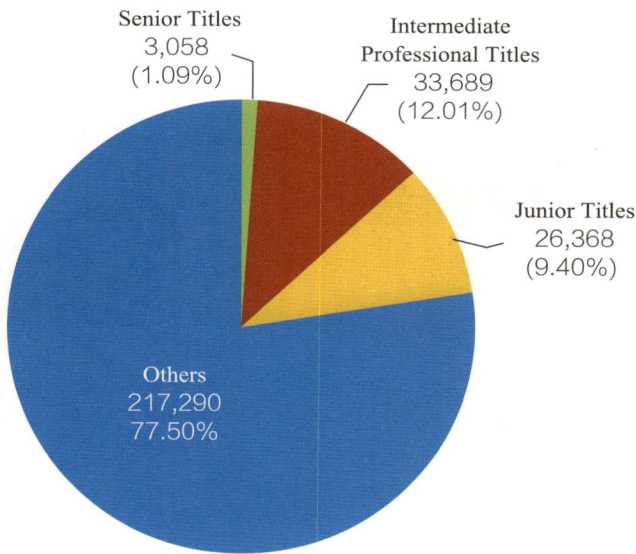

Figure 1-14   Professional titles of employees in financial institutions in Shanghai

4 Professional accreditation

19,392 (6.92%) of the employees of financial institutions in Shanghai have been accredited. About 12,200 (4.36%) have obtained a domestic certificate under the most popular and recognized professional accreditation programs, including CPA, actuaries, and financial planners. 7,192 (2.56%) have obtained an international certificate, including IOA, ChFP, CPA, AFP, CGA, FRM, CFP, CIA, ACCA, CFA, SOA, and LOMA (see Figure 1-15).

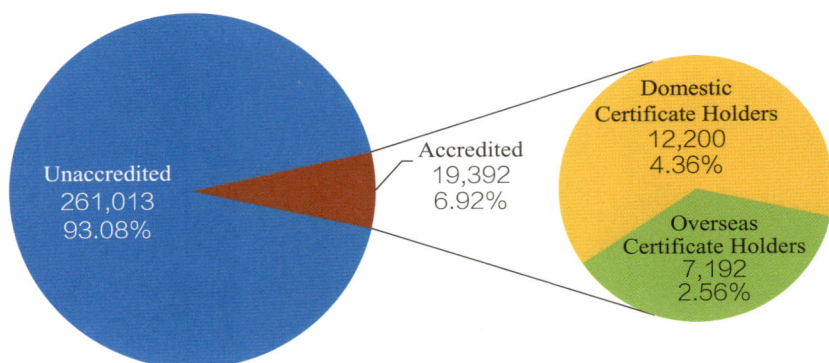

Figure 1-15　Professional accreditation of employees in financial institutions in Shanghai

85,432 (30.47%) financial employees have occupational accreditations (not including senior management qualifications) required by bank, securities and insurance regulators, such as qualifications for securities practice, qualifications for securities investment consultants, and qualifications for fund practice (see Figure 1-16).

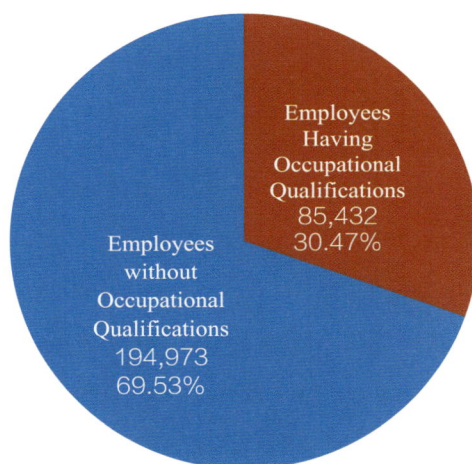

Figure 1-16　Employees of financial institutions in Shanghai having or without occupational qualifications

IV. Distribution of the financial services workforce in Shanghai

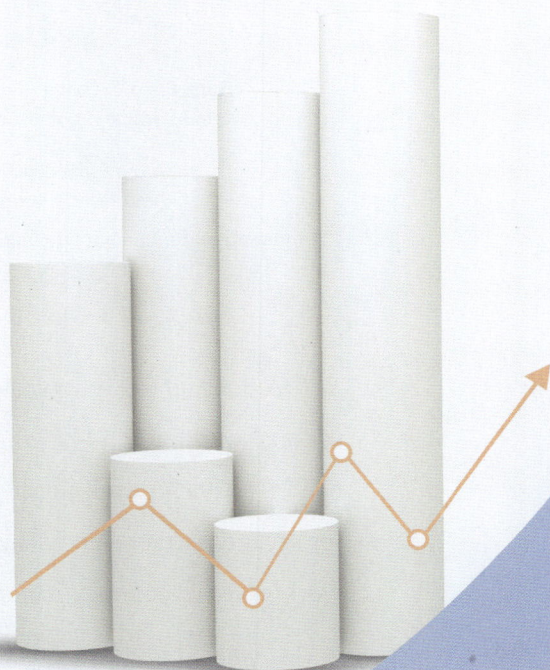

1 Breakdown by institution category

This report surveys the 328,700 financial practitioners by category to provide a clear view of the distribution of financial practitioners in Shanghai among the categories of institutions.

(1) Distribution among categories

According to the above categorization, 153,545 (46.71%) financial practitioners work for banking institutions; 68,998 (20.99%) work in the insurance category; and 61,443 (18.69%) work in the securities category. Overall, banking, insurance and securities categories have the lion's share (86.39%) of the financial services workforce (see Figure 1-17).

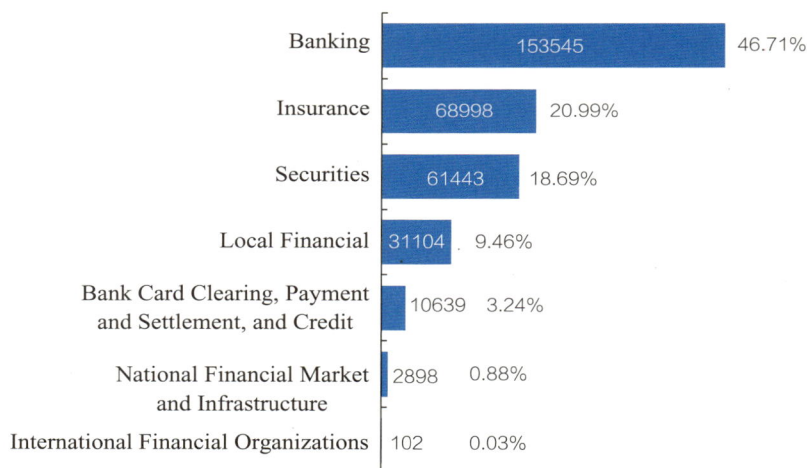

Category	Value	Percentage
Banking	153545	46.71%
Insurance	68998	20.99%
Securities	61443	18.69%
Local Financial	31104	9.46%
Bank Card Clearing, Payment and Settlement, and Credit	10639	3.24%
National Financial Market and Infrastructure	2898	0.88%
International Financial Organizations	102	0.03%

Figure 1-17   Workforce division among the seven categories

Among all the 19 sub-categories, three sub-categories claim over 10% of the total workforce: 144,137 (43.85%) work for banking institutions (banks); 68,998 (20.99%) work for insurance companies; and 37,832 (11.51%) work for securities companies. Three sub-categories have 2% to 10% of the total workforce, including financing leasing companies (7.46%), public fund companies (4.23%) and banking institutions (non-banks) (2.86%). Four sub-categories account for 1% to 2% of the total workforce: futures companies (1.91%), third-party payment institutions (1.61%), bank card clearing agencies (1.59%) and private fund managers (1.04%). Nine sub-categories have lower than 1% of the total workforce: national financial markets and infrastructure (0.88%); pawnshops (0.74%); commercial factoring companies (0.53%); micro-loan companies (0.51%); financing guarantee companies (0.14%); local asset management companies (0.05%); financial credit reporting agencies (0.03%); international financial organizations (0.03%); and regional equity markets (0.03%) (see Figure 1-18).

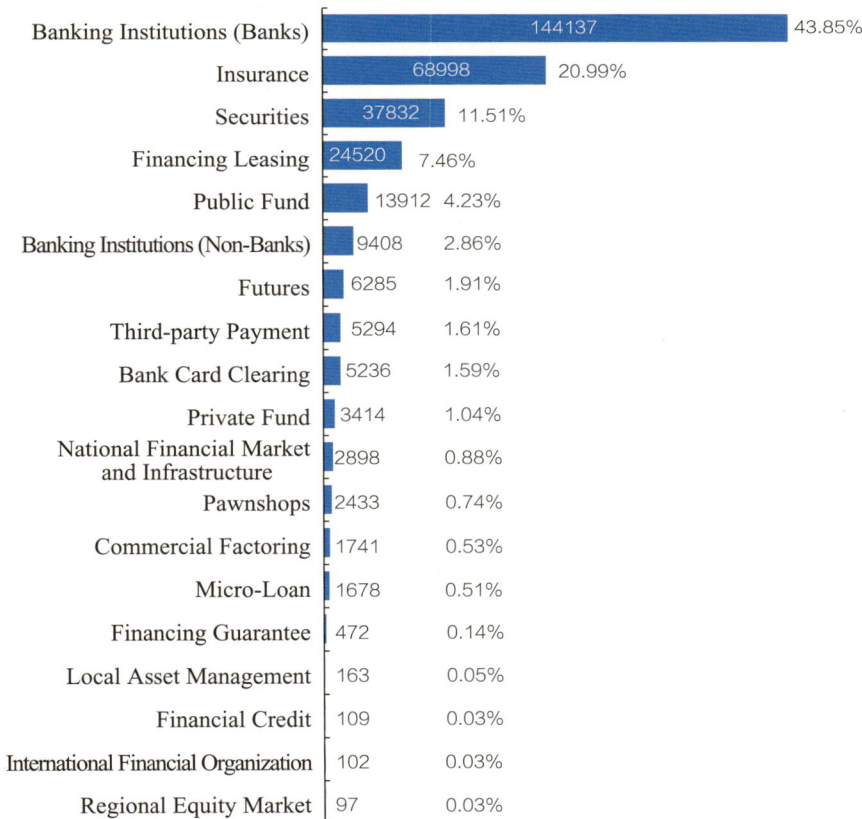

Category	Workforce	Percentage
Banking Institutions (Banks)	144137	43.85%
Insurance	68998	20.99%
Securities	37832	11.51%
Financing Leasing	24520	7.46%
Public Fund	13912	4.23%
Banking Institutions (Non-Banks)	9408	2.86%
Futures	6285	1.91%
Third-party Payment	5294	1.61%
Bank Card Clearing	5236	1.59%
Private Fund	3414	1.04%
National Financial Market and Infrastructure	2898	0.88%
Pawnshops	2433	0.74%
Commercial Factoring	1741	0.53%
Micro-Loan	1678	0.51%
Financing Guarantee	472	0.14%
Local Asset Management	163	0.05%
Financial Credit	109	0.03%
International Financial Organization	102	0.03%
Regional Equity Market	97	0.03%

Figure 1-18   Workforce division among the 19 sub-categories

(2) Gender distribution

In terms of gender distribution, banking institutions (banks) and regional equity markets hire more female practitioners than male. The former has 82,689 (57.37%) female practitioners, and the latter has 58 (59.79%). The proportion of female practitioners working for insurance institutions is 49.93%, basically at par with their male colleagues. Female practitioners working for 14 sub-categories, including securities companies, public fund companies, banking institutions (non-banks), futures companies, private fund managers, national financial markets and infrastructure, pawnshops, micro-loan companies, commercial factoring

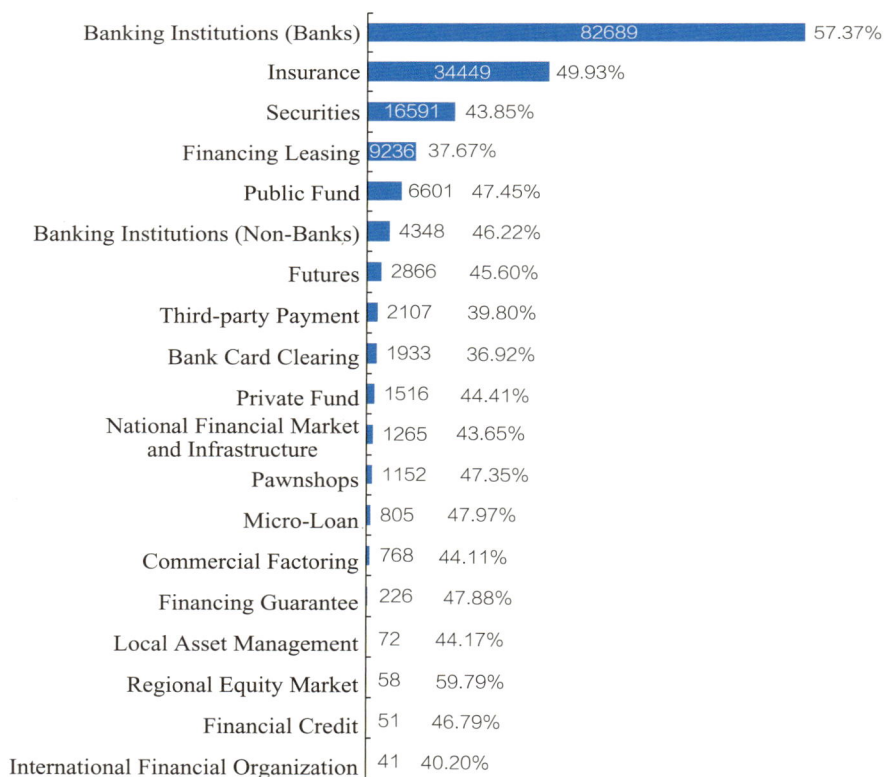

Category	Number	Percentage
Banking Institutions (Banks)	82689	57.37%
Insurance	34449	49.93%
Securities	16591	43.85%
Financing Leasing	9236	37.67%
Public Fund	6601	47.45%
Banking Institutions (Non-Banks)	4348	46.22%
Futures	2866	45.60%
Third-party Payment	2107	39.80%
Bank Card Clearing	1933	36.92%
Private Fund	1516	44.41%
National Financial Market and Infrastructure	1265	43.65%
Pawnshops	1152	47.35%
Micro-Loan	805	47.97%
Commercial Factoring	768	44.11%
Financing Guarantee	226	47.88%
Local Asset Management	72	44.17%
Regional Equity Market	58	59.79%
Financial Credit	51	46.79%
International Financial Organization	41	40.20%

Figure 1-19   Percentages of female financial practitioners by sub-category

companies, financing guarantee companies, local asset management companies, financial credit reporting agencies and international financial organizations represent 40% to 49% of the total, a bit lower than that their male counterpart. The proportion of female practitioners working for financing leasing companies, third-party payment institutions and bank card clearing institutions is less than 40% (see Figure 1-19).

(3) Practitioners from Hong Kong, Macao and Taiwan and foreign countries

There are 2,163 practitioners from Hong Kong, Macao and Taiwan and foreign countries who mainly work for banking institutions (banks), financing leasing companies and insurance institutions. Among them, banking institutions (banks) hire 585 foreigners and 514 employees from Hong Kong and Macau and Taiwan; financing leasing companies hire 41 foreigners and 272 from Hong Kong, Macao and Taiwan; and insurance institutions hire 200 foreigners and 155 employees from Hong Kong, Macao and Taiwan. In addition, a small number of practitioners from Hong Kong, Macao and Taiwan and foreign countries work for commercial factoring companies, securities companies, public fund companies, banking institutions (non-banks), futures companies, private fund managers and international financial organizations (see Figure 1-20).

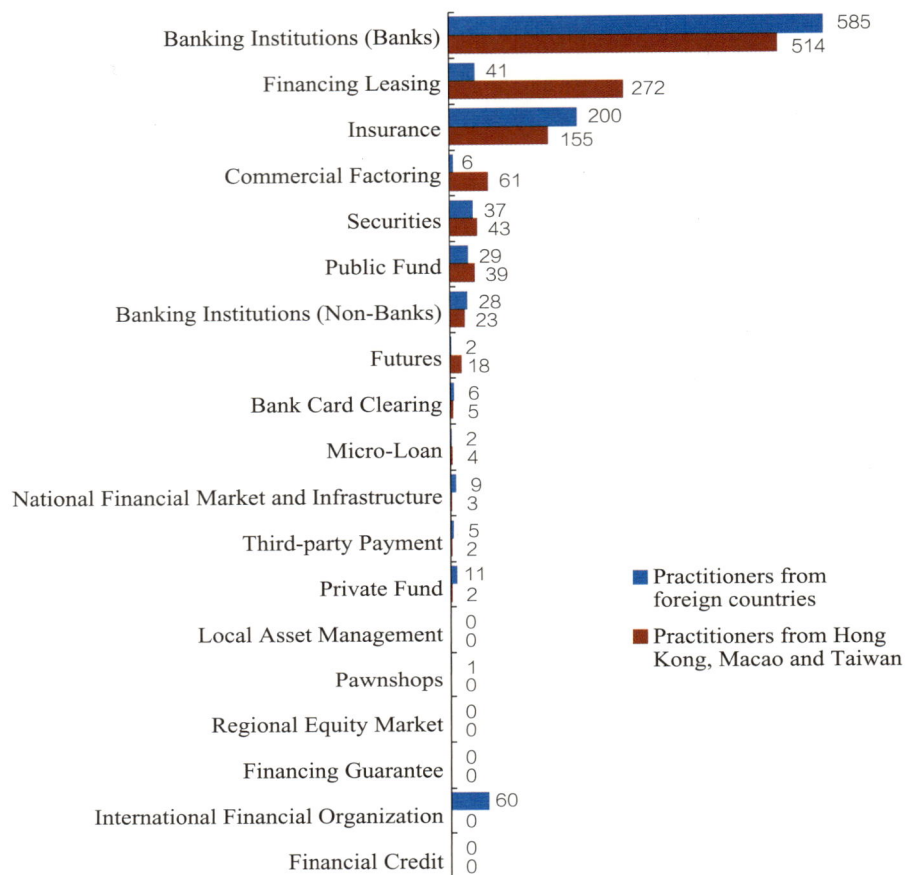

Sub-category	Practitioners from foreign countries	Practitioners from Hong Kong, Macao and Taiwan
Banking Institutions (Banks)	585	514
Financing Leasing	41	272
Insurance	200	155
Commercial Factoring	6	61
Securities	37	43
Public Fund	29	39
Banking Institutions (Non-Banks)	28	23
Futures	2	18
Bank Card Clearing	6	5
Micro-Loan	2	4
National Financial Market and Infrastructure	9	3
Third-party Payment	5	2
Private Fund	11	2
Local Asset Management	0	0
Pawnshops	1	0
Regional Equity Market	0	0
Financing Guarantee	0	0
International Financial Organization	60	0
Financial Credit	0	0

*Figure 1-20   Practitioners from Hong Kong, Macao and Taiwan and
foreign countries by sub-category*

(4) Workforce mobility

In 2017, banking institutions (banks), insurance institutions,
financing leasing companies and securities institutions topped the list
in terms of new recruits (inflow). Among them, banking institutions
(banks) recruited 25,496 practitioners, insurance institutions 16,332,
financing leasing companies 9,430 and securities companies 9,348. In
2017, the top four sub-categories in terms of workforce departure were
banking institutions (banks), insurance institutions, securities companies

and financing leasing companies. 25,306 employees left banking institutions (banks), 16,073 left insurance institutions, 8,410 left securities companies, and 5,381 left financing leasing companies. In other words, banking institutions (banks), insurance institutions, financing leasing companies and securities companies are the top four sub-categories in terms of turnover rate. Six other sub-categories also have a noticeable rate of turnover, including public fund companies, banking institutions (non-banks), futures companies, private fund managers, third-party payment institutions and bank card clearing institutions. Turnover is relatively low in nine sub-categories: national financial markets and infrastructure,

Sub-category	Departure	New recruits
Banking Institutions (Banks)	25306	25496
Insurance	16073	16332
Financing Leasing	5381	9430
Securities	8410	9348
Public Fund	2884	3020
Banking Institutions (Non-Banks)	1217	2281
Futures	1610	1854
Private Fund	2361	1248
Third-party Payment	1016	1184
Bank Card Clearing	390	1073
National Financial Market and Infrastructure	190	614
Micro-Loan	623	479
Commercial Factoring	342	411
Pawnshops	286	332
International Financial Organization	0	83
Financial Credit	38	53
Local Asset Management	18	41
Financing Guarantee	89	26
Regional Equity Market	18	16

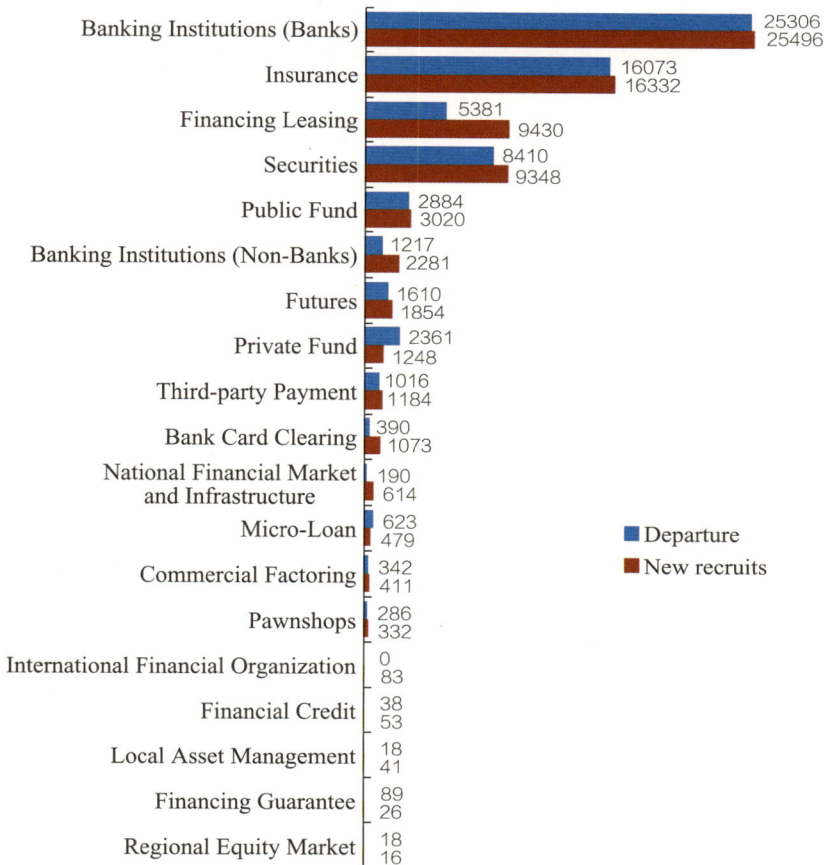

Figure 1-21   Workforce turnover by sub-category

micro-loan companies, commercial factoring companies, pawnshops, international financial organizations, financial credit reporting agencies, local asset management companies, financing guarantee companies and regional equity markets (see Figure 1-21).

In 2017, banking institutions (banks), securities companies, insurance institutions and international financial organizations recruited more practitioners from overseas, while third-party payment institutions, regional equity markets, financing leasing companies and private fund managers were lower on the list. Banking institutions, insurance institutions and national financial markets and infrastructure are the top categories in terms

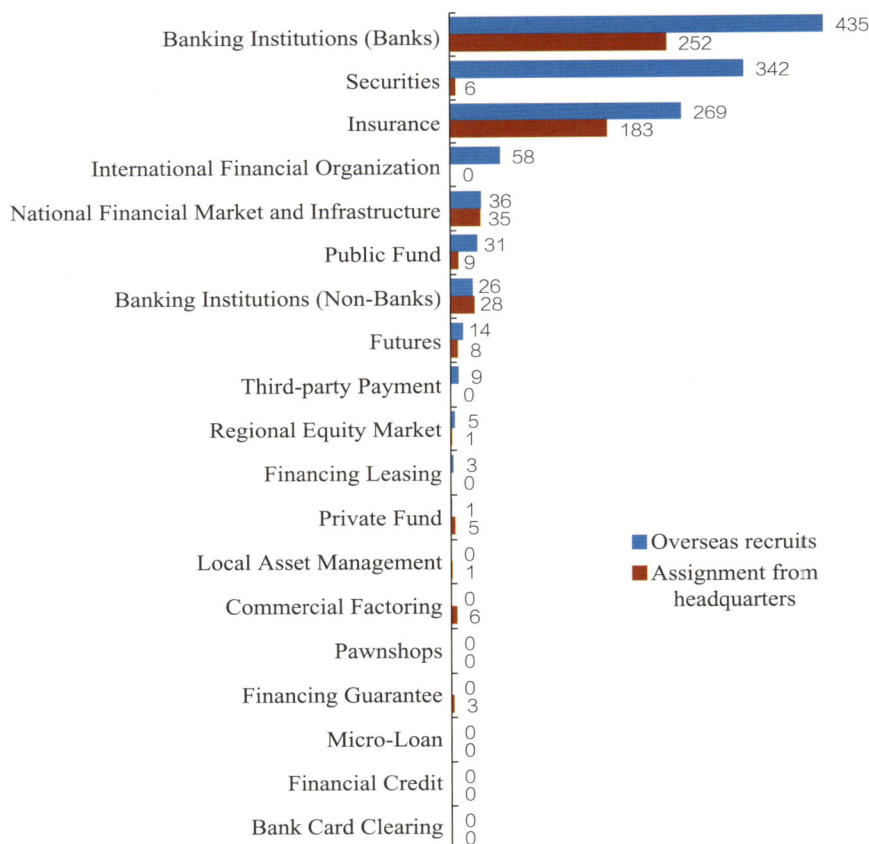

Figure 1-22   Overseas recruits and assignment from headquarters by sub-category

of assignment from headquarters (see Figure 1-22).

In 2017, banking institutions (banks), insurance institutions and securities companies were the top three sub-categories in terms of employee resignation. 21,731 practitioners resigned from banking institutions (banks), 11,837 from insurance institutions, and 6,177 from securities companies. Fewer practitioners resigned financing guarantee companies, financial credit reporting agencies, regional equity markets, local asset management companies and international financial organizations. In 2017, insurance institutions and securities companies dismissed larger numbers of practitioners, 2,147 and 1,996 respectively (see Figure 1-23).

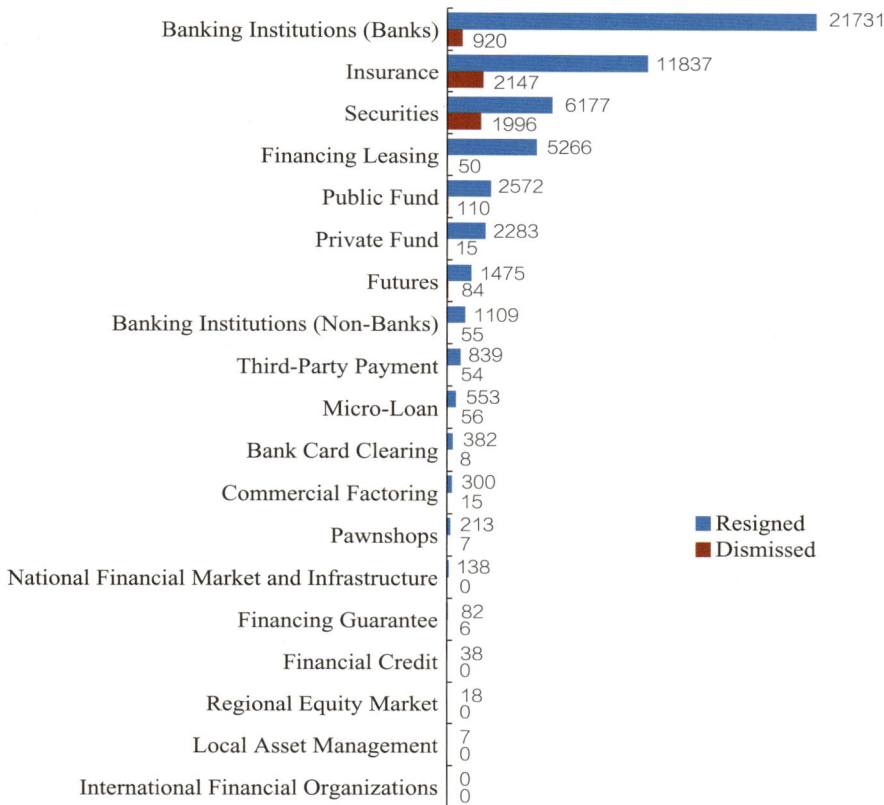

	Resigned	Dismissed
Banking Institutions (Banks)	21731	920
Insurance	11837	2147
Securities	6177	1996
Financing Leasing	5266	50
Public Fund	2572	110
Private Fund	2283	15
Futures	1475	84
Banking Institutions (Non-Banks)	1109	55
Third-Party Payment	839	54
Micro-Loan	553	56
Bank Card Clearing	382	8
Commercial Factoring	300	15
Pawnshops	213	7
National Financial Market and Infrastructure	138	0
Financing Guarantee	82	6
Financial Credit	38	0
Regional Equity Market	18	0
Local Asset Management	7	0
International Financial Organizations	0	0

Figure 1-23   Resigned and dismissed practitioners by sub-category

2 Breakdown by sub-category of institutions

As mentioned above, as of the end of 2017, financial institutions in Shanghai had 280,405 employees. There are obvious differences between sub-categories in terms of workforce age, education background, professional qualification and accreditation.

(1) Age profile

In terms of age, employees aged below 39 are over 80% of the total in ten sub-categories, including third-party payment institutions (91.92%), commercial factoring companies (91.46%), financing leasing companies (89.45%), bank card clearing institutions (88.87%), banking institutions (non-banks) (86.54%), public fund companies (86.52%), regional equity markets (84.95%), financial credit reporting agencies (81.65%), private fund managers (81.26%), and futures companies (80.56%). In five sub-categories, the percentage of employees aged below 39 is between 70% and 80%, including micro-loan companies (78.94%), securities companies (77.98%), insurance institutions (75.86%), national financial markets and infrastructure (74.23%), and banking institutions (banks) (72.75%). Pawnshops, international financial organizations, financing guarantee companies and local asset management companies have an relatively senior workforce. Employees aged 50 and above account for larger proportions: 27.05%, 14.29%, 11.74% and 10.19% respectively (see Figure 1-24).

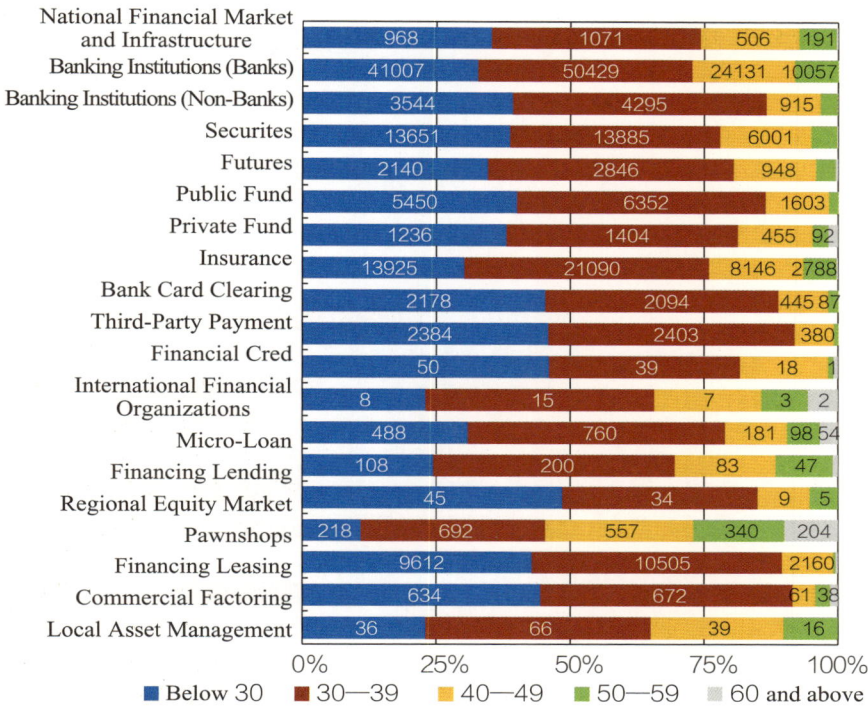

	Below 30	30—39	40—49	50—59	60 and above
National Financial Market and Infrastructure	968	1071	506	191	
Banking Institutions (Banks)	41007	50429	24131	10057	
Banking Institutions (Non-Banks)	3544	4295	915		
Securites	13651	13885	6001		
Futures	2140	2846	948		
Public Fund	5450	6352	1603		
Private Fund	1236	1404	455	92	
Insurance	13925	21090	8146	2788	
Bank Card Clearing	2178	2094	445	87	
Third-Party Payment	2384	2403	380		
Financial Cred	50	39	18	1	
International Financial Organizations	8	15	7	3	2
Micro-Loan	488	760	181	98	54
Financing Lending	108	200	83	47	
Regional Equity Market	45	34	9	5	
Pawnshops	218	692	557	340	204
Financing Leasing	9612	10505	2160		
Commercial Factoring	634	672	61	38	
Local Asset Management	36	66	39	16	

Figure 1-24　Age profile of the financial services workforce by sub-category

(2) Education background

The percentage of employees holding a Bachelor's degree is: 71.64% in commercial factoring companies; 67.95% in financing guarantee companies; 66.75% in banking institutions (banks); 62.38% in futures companies; 60.95% in financing leasing companies; 57.18% in micro-loan companies; 57.02% in banking institutions (non-banks); 54.33% in insurance institutions; and 54.07% in third-party payment institutions. The percentages of employees holding a Master's degree and a doctoral degree are: 73.53% and 2.94% in international financial organization; 63.31% and 9.39% in national financial markets and infrastructure; 54.84% and 3.23% in regional equity markets; 53.50% and 1.91% in local asset management companies; 50.16% and 0.98% in bank card clearing institutions. Employees with a junior degree (higher vocational, secondary vocational, high school and even lower diploma) are relatively concentrated in pawnshops (75.19%), micro-loan companies (28.15%), insurance institutions (26.96%) and third-party payment institutions (21.29%) (see Figure 1-25).

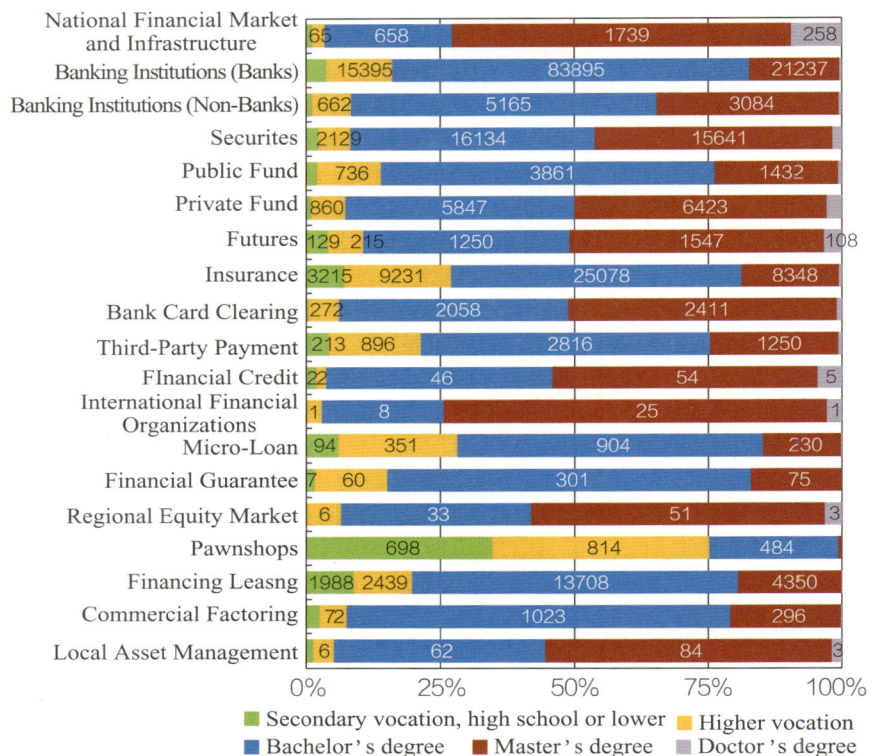

Figure 1-25　Education background of employees in financial institutions in Shanghai by sub-category

Banking institutions (banks) hire 7,885 employees holding a Bachelor's degree or an advanced degree from overseas, followed by securities companies (5,370), insurance institutions (3,112), public fund companies (2,206), financing leasing companies (2,032), banking institutions (non-banks) (1,196), futures companies (623), private fund managers (595), bank card clearing institutions (447), national financial market and infrastructure (421), third-party payment institutions (214), micro-loan companies (149), commercial factoring companies (69), financing guarantee companies (28), local asset management companies (21), regional equity markets (21), financial credit reporting agencies (19), pawnshops (11), and international financial organizations (2) (see Figure 1-26).

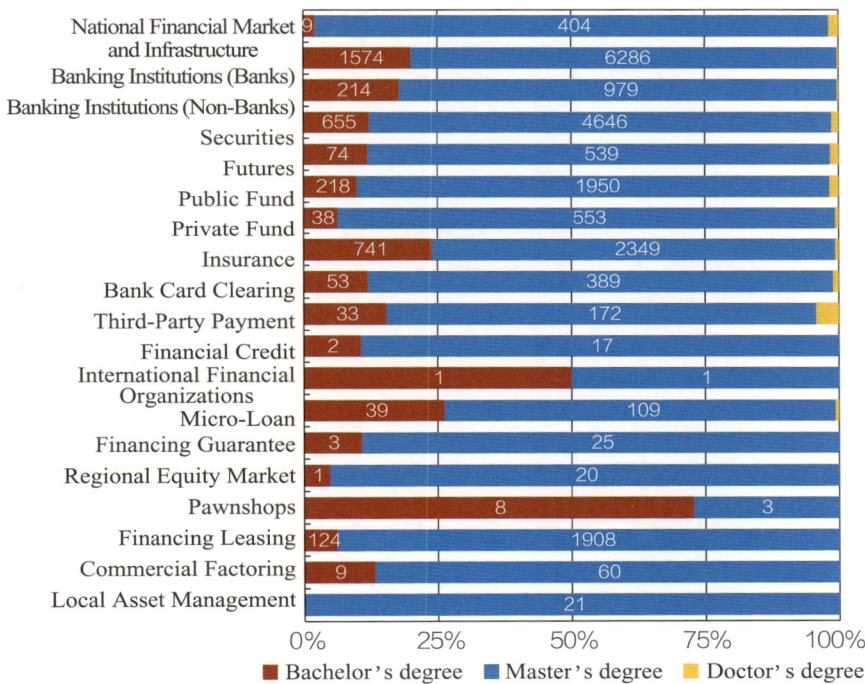

Figure 1-26 Employees in financial institutions in Shanghai with overseas education background by sub-category

(3) Professional qualifications

Employees holding a professional title are relatively concentrated in banking institutions (non-banks) (37.40%) and local asset management companies (36.31%), while 90% of employees of commercial factoring companies, financing leasing companies, international financial organizations, third-party payment institutions, insurance institutions, private fund managers and public fund managers do not have any professional title (see Figure 1-27).

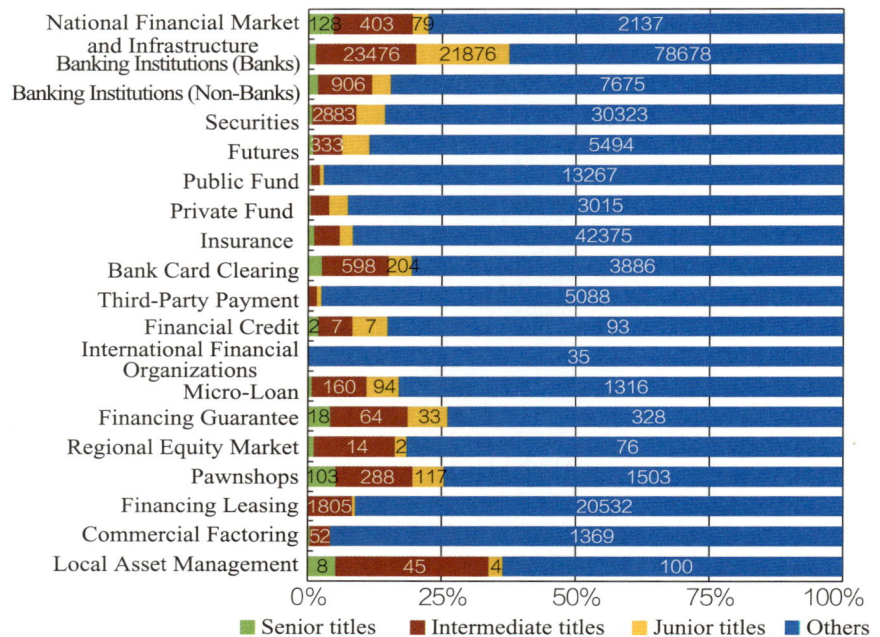

National Financial Market and Infrastructure	128 403 79	2137
Banking Institutions (Banks)	23476 21876	78678
Banking Institutions (Non-Banks)	906	7675
Securities	2883	30323
Futures	333	5494
Public Fund		13267
Private Fund		3015
Insurance		42375
Bank Card Clearing	598 204	3886
Third-Party Payment		5088
Financial Credit	2 7 7	93
International Financial Organizations		35
Micro-Loan	160 94	1316
Financing Guarantee	18 64 33	328
Regional Equity Market	14 2	76
Pawnshops	103 288 117	1503
Financing Leasing	1805	20532
Commercial Factoring	52	1369
Local Asset Management	8 45 4	100

0%   25%   50%   75%   100%

■ Senior titles ■ Intermediate titles ■ Junior titles ■ Others

*Figure 1-27   Employees of financial institutions in Shanghai
holding a professional title of by sub-category*

The percentages of employees holding a senior professional title are higher in pawnshops (5.12%) and local asset management companies (5.10%). The percentage of intermediate professional title holders in local asset management companies is 28.66%, the highest among all sub-categories. Banking institutions (banks) have a relatively high percentage (17.40%) of junior professional title holders.

(4) Professional accreditation

In terms of accredited employees, banking institutions (banks) (8,838), securities companies (4,012) and insurance institutions (3,957) top the list, with their accredited employees accounting for 7.03%, 11.36% and 8.57% of their total employees. Pawnshops, financing leasing companies, bank card clearing institutions and third-party payment institutions have lower proportions of accredited employees, which are 0.99%, 0.82%, 0.48% and 0.42% respectively (see Figure 1-28).

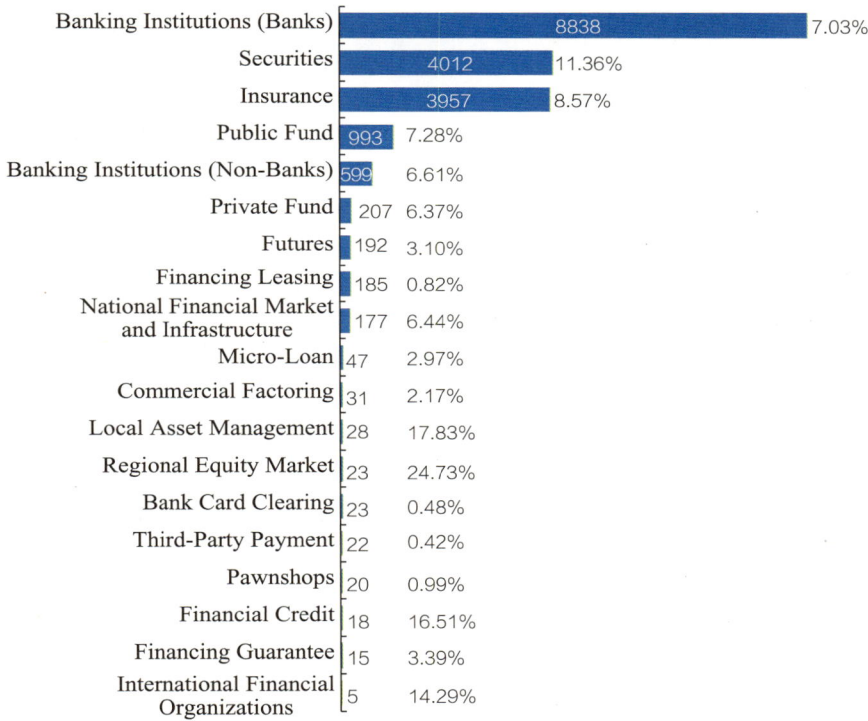

Sub-category	Value	Percentage
Banking Institutions (Banks)	8838	7.03%
Securities	4012	11.36%
Insurance	3957	8.57%
Public Fund	993	7.28%
Banking Institutions (Non-Banks)	599	6.61%
Private Fund	207	6.37%
Futures	192	3.10%
Financing Leasing	185	0.82%
National Financial Market and Infrastructure	177	6.44%
Micro-Loan	47	2.97%
Commercial Factoring	31	2.17%
Local Asset Management	28	17.83%
Regional Equity Market	23	24.73%
Bank Card Clearing	23	0.48%
Third-Party Payment	22	0.42%
Pawnshops	20	0.99%
Financial Credit	18	16.51%
Financing Guarantee	15	3.39%
International Financial Organizations	5	14.29%

Figure 1-28   Accredited employees in financial institutions in Shanghai by sub-category

The top three sub-categories having the largest number of employees holding overseas professional certificates are banking institutions (banks) (4,794), insurance institutions (829), securities companies (717). Private fund managers, national financial markets, futures companies, financing leasing companies, bank card clearing institutions, financial credit reporting agencies and local asset management companies have fewer employees holding overseas professional certificates. Commercial factoring companies, micro-loan companies and third-party payment institutions are even lower on the list. In term of employees holding overseas professional certificates as a percentage of their total, the top three sub-categories are international financial organizations (14.29%), financial credit reporting agencies (11.01%) and local asset management companies (6.37%). At the bottom end of the list are futures companies (0.71%), commercial factoring companies (0.56%), bank card clearing institutions (0.37%), financing leasing companies (0.12%), micro-loan companies (0.06%) and third-party payment institutions (0.02%) (see Figure 1-29).

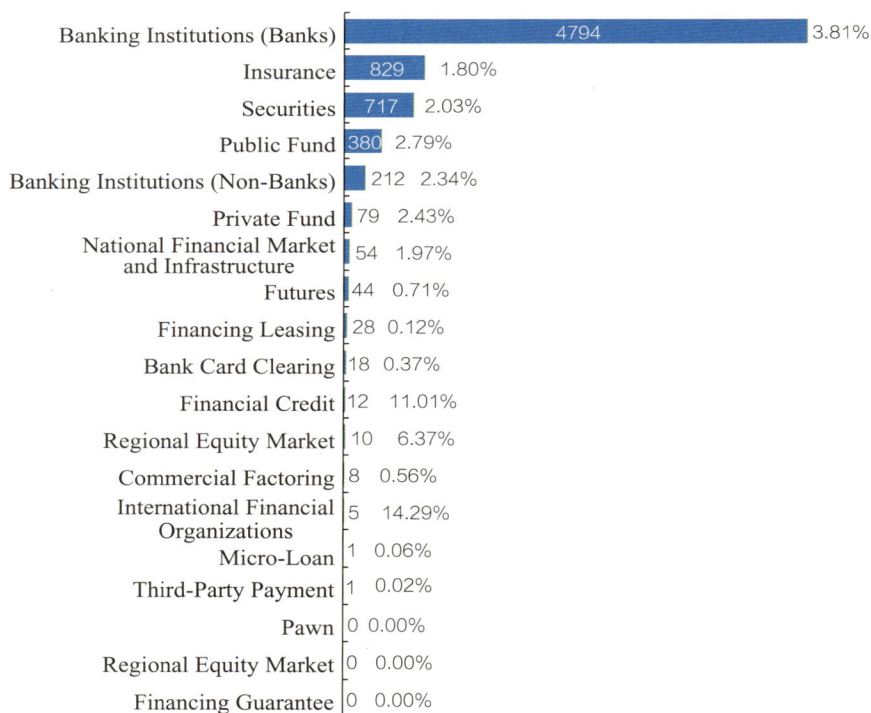

Sub-category	Value	Percentage
Banking Institutions (Banks)	4794	3.81%
Insurance	829	1.80%
Securities	717	2.03%
Public Fund	380	2.79%
Banking Institutions (Non-Banks)	212	2.34%
Private Fund	79	2.43%
National Financial Market and Infrastructure	54	1.97%
Futures	44	0.71%
Financing Leasing	28	0.12%
Bank Card Clearing	18	0.37%
Financial Credit	12	11.01%
Regional Equity Market	10	6.37%
Commercial Factoring	8	0.56%
International Financial Organizations	5	14.29%
Micro-Loan	1	0.06%
Third-Party Payment	1	0.02%
Pawn	0	0.00%
Regional Equity Market	0	0.00%
Financing Guarantee	0	0.00%

Figure 1-29   Employees holding overseas professional certificates by sub-category

图书在版编目(CIP)数据

上海金融行业从业人员统计调查报告.2018/上海
市金融工作局著.—上海:上海人民出版社,2019
ISBN 978-7-208-16066-8

Ⅰ.①上… Ⅱ.①上… Ⅲ.①金融业-从业人员-调
查报告-上海-2018 Ⅳ.①F832.751

中国版本图书馆 CIP 数据核字(2019)第 203255 号

责任编辑 马瑞瑞
封面设计 陈酌工作室

上海金融行业从业人员统计调查报告 2018
上海市金融工作局 著

出　　版　上海人人出版社
　　　　　(200001　上海福建中路 193 号)
发　　行　上海人民出版社发行中心
印　　刷　上海商务联西印刷有限公司
开　　本　787×1092　1/16
印　　张　5.5
字　　数　71,000
版　　次　2019 年 10 月第 1 版
印　　次　2019 年 10 月第 1 次印刷
ISBN 978-7-208-16066-8/F·2602
定　　价　70.00 元